MOWAT
LUANA 11/04
Fabulous —
Just what I have been
saying for 60 years

D0042232

7 MYTHS OF WORKING MOTHERS

7 MYTHS OF WORKING MOTHERS

Why Children and (Most)
Careers Just Don't Mix

SUZANNE VENKER

foreword by Dr. Laura Schlessinger

SPENCE PUBLISHING COMPANY • DALLAS

2004

Published in the United States by
Spence Publishing Company
111 Cole Street
Dallas, Texas 75207

Library of Congress Control Number: 2004100721

ISBN: 1-890626-53-8

Printed in the United States of America

For my mother,
the wisest woman I know—and the one person
I can count on to tell it like it is.

And for my children, Emma and Henry,
who make everything else pale in comparison.

It takes immense character to be able to give without recognition, to put aside the trivial material needs that seem so pressed but in reality are so trivial, to have the clearness of mind and the strength of spirit to look at what really matters and to give of yourself to make another better. And so the next time you question why the fabric of society is continuing to unravel at the edges, ask yourself what the emotional, financial, and intellectual value of motherhood is.

Michael S. Niziol

Contents

Foreword

S UZANNE VENKER is helping to lift me out of my growing despair. While my "banging the pot loudly" over the past quarter century in favor of loving, maritally-committed, two-parent, mom and dad, parent-at-home-when-children-are-home families has seen positive results—I have also witnessed, in horror and disbelief,

- parents continuing to send their children to a day care center where the owner has been arrested and indicted for negligence, abuse, breaking of state laws pertaining to child care, quoted as saying such things as, "We love her—we support her."

- the media in general, and other parents in particular, showing compassionate support and understanding to the oh-so-busy mother or father who accidentally forgot that they even had a child—a child who is no longer a burden because he cooked to death in the back seat of a car. "It could happen to anybody," is the unbelieveable response of other parents.

- the profound hostility in women's and parenting magazines to women who raise their own children, not to mention the plethora of articles that support the neglect of children as in the best interest of the child—as long as mommy is happy.

- the breakdown of basic, traditional norms, which has resulted in an almost complete loss of a sense of responsibility and obligation apart from one's own self-centered and immediate desires. Beginning with readily available contraception for use by *un*married couples to the general acceptance of abortion upon demand for no serious reason, we moved from a mentality of responsibility and obligation to a mentality in which children are disposable items. Feminists, disdaining men, marriage, and child-rearing, helped move women from a place of respect for their femininity and fertility and mothering to a place where shacking-up, out-of-wedlock babies, and day care practically wiped out their sense of specialness.

- women dumping their newborns in a trash bin to die, keeping a child abuser in their home, or murdering their children to spite their husbands, attract a new boyfriend, or relieve their emotional and psychological stress. The response of the media is overwhelming support for a woman who should be held accountable, because she was burdened by children or oppressed by the man who expected her to be a wife and mother.

- the development of products geared to make mothers feel better about abandoning their children to institutionalized day care, for the sake of the *mother's* well-being: daily charts of when and how much their child pee-ed or pooped and ate and drank, rolled over, or said some words; a camera in the day-care center so the mother can go on her computer and view her child for ten seconds. This is new-age parenting!

And just when you thought our attitudes about children couldn't get any worse, there appears a letter to the editor like this one, written by Ralph Lewis of Chesapeake, Virginia, in the *Virginia Pilot*:

In "Kudos for putting children before career" (letter, Sept. 19), Michael Julian praises a woman for letting her "career take a back seat to the most important job a person can have; raising a child."

At first glance, this seems like the right idea. But this type of thinking simply does not hold up to scrutiny. It cheapens the human experience by trapping us in a cycle.

What is the point of devoting your life to being a stay-at-home mom just so your kids can grow up and do the same thing? That contributes nothing to society as a whole. It only benefits the family unit.

Insects and animals reproduce just to be reproducing, and that is essentially what Julian is praising, whether he realizes it or not.

People have an identity outside of parenthood. That is why nannies and day-care centers exist. It is ignorant to suggest that unless you *waste your education and blindly go down the path of loud plastic toys, runny noses and juice boxes*, your livelihood and thus your life is less than that of parents.

Yes, parenthood may be nice, if that is your calling, and you can financially and emotionally support it. But please don't belittle people who aren't parents by over-glorifying an often mundane and tedious task. [Emphasis added.]

The most interesting and telling point of this letter is when Mr. Lewis talks about cheapening the human experience. And his talk of bugs and other critters shows how confused he is concerning humanness. It is in the sacrifice of raising children and fulfilling obligations to family that human beings find their glory and rise above animals. Certainly, people working on assembly lines and sitting in freeway traffic look more like ants than someone who spends her day teaching her children about God or coaching her child's soccer team.

I have a great career: I have had a private practice as a licensed marriage and family therapist, sustained a successful radio broadcasting career for a quarter of a century, and written seven *New York Times* bestselling books. I write a monthly column for WND.com, run a foundation for neglected children, create and hand-craft jewelry to raise money for the foundation, ride bicycles up and down major hills, and took up sailing. Yet I've always been an at-home mother. The writing happens at 5:00 AM, while everyone is asleep. The radio broadcasting happened first at 10:00 PM, after a full day of child care, and then shifted to middays while our son was at school. In other words, I squeezed my career in around my mothering and *not* the other way around. It can be done, if one commits to doing it right—and *right* means the child does not pay the price for the parent's ambitions and that the parent has the centering and family love that makes life a pleasure.

Upon introducing each hour of my radio program, I introduce my screener and engineer. When I get to myself—well, it's obvious I'm the host—I say, "And me, I am My Kid's Mom." It is amazing how much attention—and derision—that statement has provoked. Once, *Nightline*'s host, Ted Koppel, asked a feminist guest (I was in bed, sound asleep at the time) if she thought I said that phrase to be "provocative." Imagine! Motherhood and Apple Pie—provocative! Another time, a young college woman fresh from her "women's studies" class came to one of my book signings and asked me why I didn't introduce myself with my academic degrees. She said her class talked about me a lot (the teacher was generally insulting), and they couldn't understand why I would identify with motherhood before my accomplishments. I told her that being my son's mother and having him, as a teenager, kiss me in front of his buddies, *was* my most rewarding accomplishment. I added that I hoped her studies wouldn't warp her to the point that she would not make the choices that would lead her to have a similar reward.

Jessica, a twenty-five-year old newlywed listener of my program wrote to me:

> My husband and I are planning on having children as soon as possible. We are currently doing everything we can to get ourselves prepared financially so that I am able to stay home with our kids. I must admit that years ago, I had envisioned myself as being a working mother. Working in a corporate environment—that was what I believed the norm was. That was until I started listening to your show. I began to see your point of view and agree with

it 100%. I then started to look at the people around me. Most of the women I worked with dropped their children off at a daycare early in the morning and then had someone else pick them up and take them home. They wouldn't get to see their kids until it was dinnertime, which was too late for them to even spend any quality time with their children. It disturbed me that no one was willing to make the sacrifices that are necessary when you have kids.

While recently pursuing my company's interest, I stumbled across these "wonderful" tips for women who have absolutely no interest in raising their children. The title of the article is "Preventing Separation Anxiety." It gives women advice on how to make abandoning their children more comfortable. As you can see, the advice it offers is nothing short of disgusting. It saddens me that corporations are encouraging this type of behavior.'

Briefly, the tips include:

- Not discussing the separation with the child in advance.

- Planning ahead so you can separate from your child quickly—have all his/her things together in one bag so the separation won't be drawn out.

- When you have to walk away from your child, do so quickly and matter-of-factly.

- If separating is hard *for you*—set up opportunities to practice separating. For example, arrange to drop your child off at someone's house additional times each week until it becomes *easier for you.*

- When you pick your child up, don't be overly emotional. It's OK to act glad to see her, but don't start crying and hugging her excessively—to do so only shows your child how hard the separation was for you.

Frankly, this all sounds incredibly cruel *for the child.* But nevermind, children are an impediment to well-being, careers, acquisition, and self-fulfillment. . . . I forgot.

The *Wall Street Journal* (October 8, 2003) published a book review dealing with the impact of working mothers on the family. "The average two-income family," begins the quotation from the book, "earns far more today than did the single breadwinner family of a generation ago. And yet, once they have paid the mortgage, the car payments, the taxes, the health insurance, and the day-care bills, today's dual-income families have less discretionary income—and less money to put away for a rainy day." The reviewer points out that, "the rush of Mommies into the workplace has had the paradoxical effect of making families less secure, less flexible and poorer." The reviewer also concludes with this telling statement: "But it's weird: The authors know that having a mother at home is economically better for families. They spell it out. Nevertheless, they can't bring themselves to support of reverse migration of America's working Mommies, even if such a thing were possible. 'We remain dedicated to the best part of the feminist movement—the rock-solid belief that women who want to work should have every opportunity to do so.' Yet, if you accept their analysis, you don't have to be a male chauvinist pig to wonder: 'Um, why?'"

This leads me to *7 Myths of Working Mothers* by Suzanne Venker, who is in her mid-thirties and is herself, right now, making the personal and professional sacrifices that she urges on others. There are hundreds of books explaining why it is acceptable to leave our children in the care of strangers, but very few explaining why we would all be happier if we did not. I am grateful for this book.

Ms. Venker's contribution to humanity, to families, to marriages, to women is huge. In a way, it is sad that she's got to argue points to prove what ought to be a "given." On the other hand, her arguments are beautifully crafted and right on target for today's anti–child-rearing atmosphere. My hope for you, the reader, is that after you read this book, you will be unwavering in your commitment to do the right thing, and reap the incredible rewards.

DR. LAURA SCHLESSINGER

Acknowledgments

⁓

NOT LONG AGO, I was driving our car while my husband, Bill, sat in the passenger seat pushing the buttons on his new Palm Pilot. Foolishly, I tried to have a conversation with him. "Are you listening to me?," I asked.

"Mmm-hmm," he mumbled. The conversation—if you could call it that—went on like this for about five minutes until I realized that he hadn't heard a word I had said. I thought for a moment, and then asked, "Is this what it's been like trying to talk to me since I've been writing The Book?"

He stopped what he was doing, looked up, and very definitively said, "Yes."

Indeed, writing a book is no small task. I am sure there were many times I answered my husband in the form of a mumble, if I responded at all. Moreover, he gave up a great deal of his personal time and took over the lion's share of the household duties during the time it took me to complete this book. He also read most of the manuscript, using his keen editorial eye to greatly improve my work. Suffice it to say, I could not have written this book without him. So thank you, thank you, dear Bill, for critiquing my work and for picking up the slack at home. More important, thank you for never once questioning my ability to make this book a reality. Such faith is priceless.

Thank you Lee, Ticki, Karen, Ruthie, Jean, Sarah, and Margaret for all your help, support, and encouragement—and for listening to me go on and on about the book without once letting on that you were tired of hearing about it. And a special thank you to Ticki for her editorial advice during that very important proposal stage.

Finally, a great big thank you to my agent, Amye Dyer, whose enthusiasm equaled mine and helped me persevere. And to my editor, Mitchell Muncy, for his foresight and commitment to this issue.

7 MYTHS OF WORKING MOTHERS

Introduction

I REMEMBER THE DAYS when I awoke to an alarm clock, jumped in the shower, inhaled a bowl of cereal, gathered my things, and rushed out the door by 7:30 AM. I wouldn't see home again until about 4:30 PM, and even then I would only run in to change clothes, and then head to the gym. About an hour and a half later I'd return, take yet another shower, and then finally sit down and turn on the news. At this point my husband and I would realize we had to eat; and considering this a dreadful chore after working all day, we would prepare something that resembled an actual meal. Then we'd have to clean the kitchen. By the time we actually relaxed, the day was almost over. Perhaps we'd watch an hour or so of television or do some work for the next day, but that's about it. Truth be told, even having a conversation with one another seemed too tall an order for a weeknight.

That was then. Now I am a mother, and if I were to throw my daughter into this equation, there is no question that she, my career, my marriage, and I would all fall apart. I am not alone in this, nor am I incapable of managing such a lifestyle while other women can. No woman—no person—is capable of such balance; there just aren't enough hours in the day. Still, some women choose to believe they can have it all—raise their children and pursue a full-time career—and set out to prove it can be done. But as Ann Crittenden writes, in *The Price of Motherhood,* of career-minded baby boomers, "Those who had children soon found out that trying to compete in a race designed for the unattached was like running in a marathon with a ten-pound weight strapped to each leg."[1] Women are finally accepting the truth: being someone's mother is a full-time job.

Because of the enormous influence of the women's movement, however, society now supports the choice of mothers to pursue careers and spends most of its energy trying to help women find a balance in their lives, one that allows them to bask in their autonomy and raise children at the same time. But instead of becoming successful jugglers, women find themselves unable to keep up with the demands of their daily lives and are discontented and unfulfilled. Still, many women refuse to accept the inevitable result of trying to do it all. And when they turn to professionals for advice—particularly those in the media—they are told that their struggles are typical of most families today and that with better organizational skills, working motherhood is completely manageable.

This message is bogus.

The basic premise of *7 Myths of Working Mothers* is that raising children is a full-time job, one that dramatically alters the paths women were on prior to becoming mothers. Therefore, being successful in the workplace and at home simultaneously is impossible. This is not antifeminist, nor is it a matter of one's politics. It is just a fact. No matter how much women would like to balance work and family, the endless demands of children don't allow mothers to dedicate themselves fully to someone or something else.

I present three main arguments. First, while the choice to bring children into the world is the inherent right of every woman (and man), choosing to do so without the intention of raising them is not. If we choose to have children, we have a responsibility to raise them—regardless of which parent stays home. If this is not our intention, we should not have children. Second, if motherhood *were* viewed as the full-time job it is, it would not be considered something we could do on the side. Women would be less inclined to try and balance career and motherhood only to discover many stress-filled years later that it cannot be done. Third, those who care for other people's children on a full-time basis are not "watching" or "baby-sitting" children, as working mothers like to claim. These caregivers are *raising* other women's children. To suggest otherwise implies that all full-time mothers do all day is babysit their own children. As if all there is to motherhood is making sure our children are fed and safe. As if there isn't an enormous amount of work to be done outside of these responsibilities. The only reason working mothers don't appreciate this fact is that they have never done the work themselves.

Unfortunately, the media encourage the notion that mothers don't need to be at home. Most in the media believe that saying mothers should be home with their children means wanting to turn back the clock. They make no distinction between the antiquated idea of "a woman's place" and an honest assessment of what children need. But as Bernard Goldberg writes in *Bias,* "Reasonable people who worry about what's happening to our children are not calling for a return to the good old days, when women stayed home all day, preferably in the kitchen, preferably baking cookies. One can be in favor of women's advances and still be concerned about the attendant costs, especially when the costs are borne by children."[2] Because of the widely held belief that a mother in the home is a woman repressed, our society fails to use common sense when it comes to the working mother debate. Obviously there are some mothers, particularly single mothers or women whose husbands are struggling financially—who must go to work to put food on the table. Any thinking person understands this. But these women have very little to do with the current debate about working mothers.

"Working mother" is the term we have come up with to describe middle-class mothers who choose to work full-time for pay, and "stay-at-home mother" is the phrase we have created to describe mothers who do not work outside the home. But dividing women into these two camps has been one of our biggest mistakes, because each title is extraordinarily misleading. "Working mother" suggests the notion of a Supermom, the fictional character who magically performs two full-time jobs in the same amount of time that it takes the average woman to perform one. In reality, a working mother performs one job and *pays* other women to perform the other. "Stay-at-home mother" suggests that a mother stays home all day while her children play at her feet. In reality, she is a woman who works at home, where she performs the awesome task of raising decent, healthy, confident human beings.

Adding to the confusion is that we have no term for the mother who falls somewhere in between. Just because a mother doesn't pursue a full-fledged career—complete with time clock, commute, and nearby day care facility—doesn't mean she's out of the job market. Many mothers today work part-time or they have tremendous flexibility in their work. The common thread is that *they work around their children's needs and schedules and use a minimal amount of child care, if any.* Some own their own businesses, which allows them to come and go as they please; some work from home; some work at night or on the weekends when their children are with their father; and some work only during the hours their children are in school. Accepting motherhood as a full-time job does not mean women must be completely out of the workforce for eighteen years. It just means that for eighteen years they will have to be creative in fitting other work around their primary obligation to their children. Clearly, then, it makes no sense to pigeon-hole women as either "working mothers" or "stay-at-home mothers." We would do better to ask whether today's mothers are choosing to take primary responsibility for raising their children or are farming out their responsibility to others.

We simply must get rid of the idea that women can balance full-time careers with motherhood. Instead, we should encourage women to embrace motherhood and career separately, to plan their lives in such a way that they will be able to succeed in both of these pursuits, though at separate times. What we should be doing is telling women the truth: that most of them will experience an overwhelming feeling of love for their babies and an innate desire to protect and nurture them—to the point that it will be inconceivable to hand them over to someone else. Or that it is impossible to pursue a full-time career while raising a family if they plan to be successful at either one. Or that if they do decide to return to the workforce, they will be in for a rude awakening when they begin their search for someone to replace them at home.

In the meantime, the conflict between full-time mothers and working mothers will continue—despite the assertion that women should be united in supporting one another's "decision"—because there is a fundamental difference in their views of motherhood. While full-time mothers refuse to relinquish the control, responsibility, and gift of raising their own children, working mothers seem to feel that their choice to be away from their children all day, every day somehow makes them a better parent—when all it really does is keep them from being a parent at all. It is my hope that, in reading this book, women begin to look at motherhood differently. The way in which children are raised has everything to do with who they become, how they function in school and society, and how successful they will be in their future relationships. More important, it is my hope that women will come to value *raising*, not having, children—whether or not society decides to support them for the work they do. After all, it shouldn't really matter what society thinks; what should matter is what we know in our hearts to be right.

Our careers can wait.

"Men Can Have It All.
Why Shouldn't We?"

Women who now leave their families every morning
to board commuter trains—the women who have
traded in their housecoats for business suits, vacu-
ums for computers, demanding, tantrum-throwing
children for demanding, tantrum-throwing col-
leagues—may well wonder if they haven't simply
traded in one form of unhappiness for another.

It is at this intimate level that feminism has
failed women.

Danielle Crittenden

I F YOU ASK THE AVERAGE PERSON to define feminism, don't expect a long-winded answer. Most people will tell you it has
something to do with the time when women banded together
to demand that they be treated as men's equals. You know, women's
rights and equal pay for equal work—that sort of thing. But chances
are they won't be able to tell you what feminism stands for or what
effect it has had because, quite frankly, they don't really know. And
their confusion is valid. After all, there's feminism—and then there's
what feminism has become.

Most women (and men, actually) are feminists. Even if you don't consider yourself a feminist—and I can understand why you wouldn't—you probably are. Simply put, a feminist is a person who believes that women are inherently equal to men and should therefore have the same opportunities that men do. A feminist also accepts that, like men, women have free will and can therefore never be victims simply by virtue of being female. Most important, a feminist takes into account the male point of view on every social issue, even matters related to children, because a true feminist knows that since the sexes are inherently equal, the voice of one sex can never dominate the other.

Some of the best-known feminists of our time had the misfortune of living in an era in which women were viewed as second-class citizens and were therefore treated as such. As a result, women took it upon themselves to fight for their rights—and they succeeded. Thanks to them, you and I enjoy rights that should have been ours to begin with, rights that women in previous generations could only dream about: the right to vote, the right to compete in the workplace, and the right to equal pay for equal work. As Christina Hoff Sommers writes in *Who Stole Feminism?,* "American women owe an incalculable debt to the classically liberal feminists who came before us and fought long and hard to gain for women the rights that the men of this country had taken for granted for over two hundred years."[1] Today, women no longer need men specifically for the purpose of being supported or recognized in their own right. *These* are the issues on which real feminism was based.

Unfortunately, mixed in with this group of pioneers was an even more vocal group, those who would eventually become the leaders of what we now call "the women's movement." Their agenda was far more extreme and would eventually become the boilerplate of modern-day feminism. The basic goal of this group is to persuade women that they are victims of patriarchal oppression, that they are handicapped because of their femaleness in virtually every social arena. Moreover, they do not wish to hear men's voices at all—unless, of course, it's for the purpose of supporting their agenda. Sommers was the first to give a name to this group of women, one that would separate them from real feminists. She calls them "gender feminists,"[2] and for the purpose of clarity, I will borrow her phrase for the remainder of the book.

Gender feminists do not speak for the majority of women: "On the contrary, their divisive and resentful philosophy adds to the woes of our society and hurts legitimate feminism."[3] Gender feminists believe in a very different kind of equality, one that goes far beyond reason and common sense. They don't merely argue for a woman's right to choose the course of her own life or for men and women to be treated equally in the workplace, they want men and women to be treated as though they are exactly the same, as though biological differences have no implications.

When the women's movement was in its heyday, its leaders didn't describe their philosophy in this way. Indeed, one of the reasons Betty Friedan, a founder of the National Organization for Women (NOW), won the support of so many women in the 1960s was that her organization appeared merely to support the idea that men and women should be treated equally. And who could argue with that? What many women did not realize—*could* not have realized—is that this supposedly simple philosophy would one day wreak havoc on motherhood. After all, if society were to make no distinctions between men and women, there could be no accommodation made for the fact that women bear children. And if there were no such accommodation, then society could not encourage or support women in the pursuit of full-time motherhood. Every man and woman would be expected to earn an income, and children would not be raised in their own homes by their own parents, but would instead grow up in government-subsidized child care programs or in the care of come-and-go nannies.

And, as it turns out, that's exactly what happened.

But the women's movement went even further. Despite asserting that its platform was all about "choice," it simultaneously belabored the notion that full-time motherhood is not a worthy ambition, that children drag women down, and that women can only find true satisfaction in the workplace. Even now, women's groups state proudly and matter-of-factly that if women want to maintain their true identities, they must be financially independent of men and freed from the shackles of childrearing. As Carolyn Graglia writes in *Domestic Tranquility,* "Women, assert feminists, should treat children as relatively independent appendages to their life of full-time involvement in the workplace. To live what feminists assure her is the only life worthy of respect, a woman must devote the vast bulk of her time and energy to market production, at the expense of children. Children, she is told, are better cared for by surrogates."[4]

This philosophy is most clear in the words of Betty Friedan, who became famous for identifying "the problem that has no name" in *The Feminine Mystique,* first published in 1963—before some of us were even born. (An updated version was released in 2001.) The "problem" is the plight of the 1950s housewife—the bored, frustrated mother who cannot escape the prison of her home. Most women today have carved out paths of their own prior to motherhood and can empathize with the women of that time who felt "stuck." Unfortunately, Friedan's message was not about supporting a woman's right to choose a career before or instead of raising a family, nor was it about equal pay for equal work. It was about encouraging women to leave their children behind in search of greener pastures. It was about demeaning and degrading the most important and valuable work women will ever do: raise their children.

Of course, the women's movement will deny that its platform is about anything other than choice. But look at what's happened over the past forty years. In the introductory section of the updated *Feminine Mystique,* Friedan writes that in the 1950s, women were defined solely in terms of their sexual relation to men: "man's wife, sex object, mother, housewife."[5] She writes that this image—which she names "the feminine mystique"[6]—was so widespread that women's magazines, movies, television commercials, mass media, and textbooks all glorified her role in a way that made women who didn't "have an orgasm waxing the kitchen floor"[7] feel alone and aberrant in their desire to get more out of life. Now compare that image with what we see today in women's magazines, movies, television commercials, mass media and textbooks: the glorification of the working mother. Almost every television program today portrays a mother who is in the workforce, despite having children at home, and commercials are all geared toward the life of working mothers. Moreover, newspaper headlines repeatedly use the words *balance, day care, family-friendly, juggle,* and *stress* to suggest that the majority of mothers are now in the workforce full-time. Indeed, the pendulum has swung so far in the opposite direction that now women feel alone and aberrant in their desire to be home with their children. Clearly, then, the women's movement was about far more than honoring the idea of choice. As Midge Decter writes in *An Old Wife's Tale*, "What [feminists] demanded was not a chance to compete fairly but to turn the whole world upside down so as to make it more suitable for them."[8] Indeed, it wasn't equality that Freidan was after. What she really wanted was to pretend that most women are not biologically wired to want to raise children, that most women can be fulfilled only in the workforce, not at home with their children, where they are "lulled into a false sense of anonymous security in their comfortable concentration camps."[9] It appears, however, that self-fulfillment is not all Friedan said it would be, since forty years later the majority of women still choose to be home with their children. "Mothers have not abandoned home and hearth to go to 'work.' The majority of American mothers are still primarily engaged in the oldest economy in the world: the household," writes Ann Crittenden.[10] This is a surprise to many people, for the media would like us to believe that this isn't true. But it is.

The single greatest problem with the women's movement is that it was predicated on the notion that women should be able to have it all. As Marlo Thomas said to Phil Donahue in the 1970s, "Men can have it all. Why shouldn't we?"[11] This philosophy would send women into the workforce permanently, as if it were unnecessary for women to give motherhood any thought, as if when women do become mothers, children should only be a temporary distraction from their career plans. But such an argument can be made only by those who have never done the work of motherhood (and Thomas never did have children), because once women have done this work, they see for themselves how absurd this idea is. Motherhood is not only a full-time job, it is *all-consuming*. The needs of children are endless.

Of course, part of the problem lay in Thomas's misguided analysis of men's lives. It is simply inaccurate to suggest that men have it all. Like today's working mothers, most fathers pursue full-time employment and merely engage in peripheral parenting. This is hardly the same as "having it all," a phrase that suggests that a person pursues a career and raises children at the same time. As Tara Fisher, a former working mother, observes, "I didn't know my children very well before. I saw them only at their worst time. I would get home at dinnertime. I would cram food into their mouths, and I would put them to bed. I never got to see the good moments, only the tired, cranky ones. Now I get to hear the genuine laughter of being a kid."[12] Certainly the average father can understand this, for he also is used to being away from his children during the important moments of their lives: their first steps, their first words, their first laugh. I am sure that most fathers—at least the good ones—would rather be present for these milestones than sitting at their desks at work. As one father tells Sylvia Ann Hewlett, "Thinking back on it, I know I didn't have children the way my wife had children. I didn't get to take them out for hot chocolate after school or hang out with their friends. To this day I have no idea what music they like or whether they're afraid of death. I see this as a permanent loss, the price I paid for an absorbing career."[13] Indeed, the reality is that the parent in the workforce will always be less involved with the children. It seems obvious that Thomas and her contemporaries have been chasing a dream that none of us, male or female, has ever achieved—or ever will achieve.

Since the women's movement first took hold of American society, women have given "having it all" their best shot. Thankfully, many have given up. Not only have they experienced what the philosophy has done to children and families, they realize that they were misled. As Lisa Schiffren writes, "My generation grew up accepting the truth of this view; many of us have been surprised to find childrearing so rewarding."[14] Indeed, women have learned several truths about motherhood. First, a woman's identity *is* inextricably linked to her children's; working outside the home does not make this any less true. Second, women miss their children when they are away from them and begin to wonder what is the point of having children if it is not to be with them most of the time. (Isn't this why people *have* families?) Lastly, women realize that their career ambitions have nothing to do with their desire to raise children. Being at home does not mean they do not want to be successful in the workplace; it just means they can't do both at the same time.

It's too bad women didn't quit while they were ahead, because the genesis of the women's movement made perfect sense: Of course women should feel free to make their own choices; of course workplace discrimination is wrong; of course men need to be involved in parenting. But to suggest that women should remain in the workforce their entire lives to prove something to themselves and the world at their children's expense is simply wrong. Friedan was right that women should not be expected to spend their entire lives focused only on the needs of their families—particularly before they've had a chance to focus on themselves—but this doesn't mean that when women do have children, they have a "right" to leave their children to be raised by others. Moreover, the concept of choice—that which gender feminists hold dear—is highly overrated, for the more choices one has in life, the more complicated things become. "Too many people seem to forget, or perhaps have never understood in the first place, that blessings can also be something of a burden," writes Decter.[15] With so much freedom and choice surrounding career and motherhood, women have been unable to set boundaries for themselves and therefore have a difficult time with any decision they make. Those who hope to have children after they reach a certain level of success in the workplace find themselves disappointed when their visions of motherhood begin to fade, and women who attempt to raise families while they spend the majority of their time and energy pursuing careers suffer a great deal of guilt and stress as a result. As Peggy Orenstein found in her interviews with over one hundred women across the country, many women are now apprehensive about their futures. One woman tells her, "You know, sometimes I wonder if we'd be happier living in a society where there weren't so many choices."[16] This is not to suggest that women shouldn't have choices or that women should marry and have children at a young age. But women cannot escape the fact that their decision to postpone motherhood—aside from the obvious biological implications—will create inner turmoil when they decide they *are* ready to have children. Not only will it be hard for them to drop everything they have worked so hard for to pursue something entirely unrelated, they may find themselves wanting to be home with their children and questioning this most basic desire. *This* is the true damage of the women's movement.

Kristen

Unfortunately, gender feminists are still among us, as Susan Douglas and Meredith Michaels demonstrate in their new book, *The Mommy Myth*. The authors claim that the state of motherhood in America has once again resorted to its 1950s ideal: the unrealistic expectation that women can or should be happy at home raising children. Simply put, they are angry that the majority of women have been taken in by what they call the "idealization of motherhood"—a situation that has occurred, they claim, because of media images that are thrust upon women. Rather than recognize that women simply prefer to be their children's primary caregivers, Douglas and Michaels exhume the message of the women's movement: "It is important that we remind ourselves of the tyranny of the role of the MRS, because it was what feminists attacked as utterly oppressive, and because, under the guise of the new momism, it has risen, pheonixlike, and burrowed its way once again into the media and into the hearts and minds of millions of mothers."[17]

The supporters of the women's movement have motherhood all wrong. They are correct that becoming full-time mothers causes women to lose the identities they once had. But what they do not appreciate is that who women become as a result of being full-time mothers is far richer than who they would have become had they not become mothers. As Anna Quindlen writes, "My children have been the making of me as a human being."[18]

~

"I Could Never Stay Home Full-Time."

"Mommy, I don't want you to work. Why can't you
be more like Joey's mom? She stays home with
him."

"Well, maybe that's because Joey's mother can't
do anything else."

ouch!

Judging Amy

N O WOMAN IN AMERICA TODAY who starts her search for identity can be sure where it will take her," writes Friedan at the
close of *The Feminine Mystique*.[1] The year was 1963. So here
we are, forty years later. And just exactly where has the search taken
us? Motherhood has been officially demoted from the top rung of
the ladder to the bottom, and in its place is the all-important career.
Women now spend all of their time and energy—all of it—preparing
for a life at the office rather than for a life at home. In fact, women's
"search for identity" has become so myopic that many women almost
forget to *have* children. Nature has to knock on their doors before
they realize how much time has passed. And those who manage to
conceive—despite their aging eggs—do not bask in their newfound

status but instead confront the Big Decision: whether to stay home with their children or return to the workforce.

Naturally, most women feel an immediate tug in the direction of home. There is, after all, something magical that takes place the moment a baby is placed in our arms. The problem, unfortunately, is that modern-day society suggests it's unnatural, even abnormal, for women to want to stay home and take care of their own babies. "Any strong rush of maternal feeling, any desire to surrender pieces of our professional selves, is viewed as a reversion to some stereotype of motherhood the women's movement was supposed to have emancipated us from," writes Danielle Crittenden in *What Our Mothers Didn't Tell Us*.[2] Thus, women begin to question the value of full-time motherhood—despite knowing they shouldn't, somewhere deep within their psyches. Sadly, the working mother trend overpowers any maternal awakening these women might have. "Most people, especially young people, need to be confirmed by the community in which they live. They cannot beyond a certain limit establish for themselves a system of their own verities and preferences," writes Midge Decter.[3] As a result, many women decide to jump on the bandwagon, when in truth they would love permission to get off. Suffice it to say, today's women are no less conflicted about where they belong than women were forty years ago. Their "search for identity" continues.

Only now the expectations are reversed.

And this is perhaps the greatest tragedy of modern-day society. Because our society encourages mothers to "go to work," women choose to forgo the greatest opportunity of their lives. How sad that any one of us could allow our choices regarding motherhood to be governed by an outside force, that we would give up an entire portion of our lives—the most valuable portion of our lives—because we believe everything we're told about full-time motherhood. It would seem to make far more sense to give motherhood a try before deciding how we feel about it. But too many women now make up their minds about whether to stay home with their children even before they become mothers. They don't even consider full-time motherhood an option, as indicated by one of the most popular phrases of the past decade: "Oh, I could never stay home full-time." Women who say this make a great assumption about motherhood, for they cannot really know how they feel about being at home with children because they never have been. Moreover, this all-too-famous cliche suggests that spending a lot of time with one's children is somehow a bad thing. "It amazes me that women say this as though [being with one's children] were a punishment," says one former working mother.[4] Maternity leave is nothing but a glimpse of the life that awaits a woman. What she experiences during this time is a mere fraction of what she will experience over the coming years. But the average new mother can't appreciate this.

That's what happened to Laurie Tennant, who says that her life as a working mother seemed to be working out fine: "I felt perfectly balanced."[5] It wasn't until her second child came, when she was home on another maternity leave, that she had the opportunity to spend a considerable amount of time with her first child, who was by then several years older. She was "jolted by how much she enjoyed the experience."[6] Shortly thereafter, Tennant quit her job. There is no way for a woman to know in advance whether she can stay home full-time.

I remember a conversation I had with a friend of mine who is thirty-six, single, and owns her own business. During the course of the conversation, she mentioned that one of her employees had recently become a full-time mom. She said she was surprised that this woman had made the choice to stay home because she did not seem like the "type." I asked her what she meant by this; and she replied, "Well, it's just that she has so much energy that I can't picture her at home all day." My friend doesn't see the irony in her statement, but this "energy" she assumes is unnecessary is precisely what motherhood demands. As I later pondered our conversation and thought about similar discussions I've had with other women, most of whom were not yet mothers, I realized that motherhood is the most elusive profession in the world. It is the one job for which we cannot see the work as it's being done, nor can we necessarily assess our progress. Thus, it is impossible to quantify the work the way we do other jobs. As Ann Crittenden writes, "Like the work of a fine seamstress, tiny stitches that build character and confidence are invisible to the naked eye."[7]

All mothers know that it is futile to try and convey to the casual observer what their job is like. A woman who does not have children could easily sit with a group of mothers and children and watch as the mothers wipe away a few tears, change a couple of diapers, or discipline their children—and wonder what could be so difficult about motherhood. Or she could observe a mother casually walking her baby in a stroller and believe she understands why some women refer to motherhood as "boring." What she will not appreciate is the work that takes place when no one else is looking. If I were not with my daughter every day, it would be impossible for me to understand exactly how she gains a feeling of self-worth by hearing my voice and seeing my face throughout the day—in the same manner, within the same routine. It would be impossible for me to understand the effect of my presence as she climbs a step and turns to see if I'm there before she moves to the next one. It would be impossible for me to appreciate her ability to make connections between what I say and what I do and how this leads to her intellectual growth. It would be impossible for me to understand how my being there to encourage her to keep trying each time she thinks she can't do something will help mold the person she later will become. It would be impossible for me to appreciate how important discipline is—that it be taught by me, her mother, every day, in the same manner—so she is not confused by the methods of numerous caregivers. It would be impossible for me to understand how vital it is that I am present each day to see that she stays on a routine, eating and sleeping well and avoiding sickness when possible. It would be impossible for me to appreciate how much she needs me when she is sick or tired or sad or bored. Those who are not there *every day* to see exactly how parenting works can never truly appreciate its value.

For this reason, many husbands, working mothers, and women without children constantly wonder what it is that full-time mothers *do*. And when they do not get a satisfactory answer, as they never will, they succumb to seven further myths about full-time motherhood. These myths have officially sunk into our collective psyche. We just can't seem to accept that motherhood is a fulfilling and noble endeavor. Indeed, the thought of raising the children we bring into this world is no longer *felt* to be an inherent responsibility, but is viewed as our choice to do or not do.

Working motherhood has become accepted as a fact of life. If we want to take control of our lives, we must begin to think independent of those around us and not blindly accept what we are told. We simply must debunk the myths about full-time motherhood that have infected our culture.

Myth #1

The majority of mothers today are "working mothers."

The thing to remember when you hear a statistic reported on the news is that what it means and how it's portrayed are two very different things. The media doesn't sift through the fine print for you; you have to do this yourself or you will be misled. But since most people don't have time to seek the details on their own, they take the media at their word. Unfortunately, the media wants you to believe that when it comes to motherhood, just about every woman in this country is now a working mother, but this isn't true. Here are the real figures, according to the United States Census Bureau:

For families with children *under age eighteen*:

- Moms employed full-time and year-round: 39.8 percent ("working mothers")
- Moms employed part-time: 34.3 percent
- Moms not employed: 25.9 percent

For families with children *under age six*:

- Moms employed full-time and year-round: 36.3 percent ("working mothers")
- Moms employed part-time: 37.1 percent
- Moms not employed: 26.6 percent[8]

Clearly, the stereotypical "working mother" we hear so much about—the woman who pursues a full-time career and places her children in someone else's care—is in the *minority*. The reason the media is able to manipulate the statistics is that they do not distinguish mothers who work ten hours a week out of their homes while their children are asleep and those who work sixty hours a week while their children are in day care or with a nanny. Thus, the media can report, as *Child* magazine did recently, that "70% of moms"[9] now juggle career and family, because if you add the mothers who work both part-time and full-time, you will come up with this figure. A mother who brings home an income of even *one dollar* is viewed as a working mother. Since I am a writer, for example, I am considered a working mother. The fact that I "work" intermittently—some days I do, some days I don't, and when I do my daughter is usually sleeping or with her father—is somehow irrelevant. The fact that months or even years could go by before I am at the computer again is also irrelevant. (This is a work pattern known as "sequencing," a term coined by Arlene Cardozo in her 1986 book of that title.) Regardless of how sporadic my income is and regardless of the fact that I do not use nannies and day care, I am still considered part of the "majority of mothers . . . now in the workforce." Yet anyone who knows me would certainly describe me as a full-time mother.

It is also interesting to note the breakdown of the care non-school age children receive. Almost *a full 50 percent of mothers* are non-employed, and another 12.3 percent is comprised of full-time dads (1 percent), moms who work beside their children (3 percent), and tag-team arrangements (7.8 percent), where mom and dad provide alternate care in different shifts. This means that 74.6 percent of non-school-age children under the age of five are in their family's care, while only 25.4 percent are cared for on a full-time basis by someone other than their family. (This alternative care consists of institutional day care—15.1 percent—in-home day care—8 percent—and nannies—2.4 percent.) Clearly, these statistics do not confirm the media's image of today's mother. The reality is that there are *far* fewer mothers choosing to pursue careers than Americans are led to believe.

The result of this myth is that many women assume that the majority of children are not being cared for by their mothers and fear that if they choose to stay home and raise their children, they will be left to venture the seas alone. As Collette Leskovyansky describes it, "I think that what the media has accomplished for me is to infuse a sense of despondency about becoming a mother."[10] It is vital that women like Leskovyansky know that the majority of mothers in this country *are* full-time mothers. We may know them as "stay-at-home mothers" or mothers "who work a little on the side," but the actual definition of a full-time mother is a woman who makes her children her priority, and any other interests she pursues—paid or unpaid—are tailored to her children's needs.

Myth #2
Stay-at-home mothers are traditional types,
and working mothers are liberated.

Let's get one thing straight: *All mothers work.* The definition of work is *physical or mental effort or activity directed toward the production or accomplishment of something.* The dictionary lists a total of thirteen definitions, only one of which refers to money. Clearly there is work we all do—housework, yard work, errand running, exercising—that has no monetary value but still constitutes work. It's a matter of what we choose to value. Anyone who doesn't see that raising children is work simply doesn't value children. Period. It is absurd to attribute the word *work* to only one of these two groups of women.

But the single greatest problem with the phrase *stay-at-home mom* is that it immediately conjures an image of the 1950s housewife. Meghan Cox Gurdon, a radio correspondent turned full-time mom, writes about how today's women were taught to view motherhood: "If there was any occupation less hip, less relevant, I for one could not imagine what it was. Housewives wore polyester chintz housedresses, baked bundt cakes in their ranch homes, and then drove station wagons to PTA meetings. They were dull, unsexy, fretted over trivialities, and lived vicariously through their husbands and children in order to compensate for their own pathetic incompleteness." At least, that was the thinking in 1964, "a year after Betty Friedan published *The Feminine Mystique*," writes Gurdon.[11]

And yet, few full-time mothers know anyone who even remotely resembles this caricature: "Wander into any Starbuck's in the hours after the commuters are gone. See all those mothers watching over toddlers at play? If you look past the Lycra gym clothes, the scene could be the 50's, but for the fact that the coffee is more expensive and the mothers have MBA's."[12] Indeed, today's average mother has spent many years in the workforce before becoming a mother. She is therefore no less educated or knowledgeable about the "working world" than her working mother friend. This was not the case in our parents' generation. "[Full-time moms] are not bored, foolish, or frustrated," writes Gurdon. "We wear jeans, miniskirts, and leggings and talk politics as much as we do infant-feeding schedules."[13] The problem is that the title *stay-at-home mom* propels women back to a bygone era, but not only are full-time mothers home by choice, rather than expectation, most do not spend their days inside the home, since modern conveniences and mobility have now freed women to enjoy life more. They are out and about with other women and children—at the gym, at storytime, or at playgroups. It makes more sense to refer to these women as full-time mothers, since you may find it hard to reach them at home.

The term *working mother* is misleading as well. It conjures an image of a woman who manages to work at a full-time career while performing the work of motherhood simultaneously. She's amazing, we say! Just how does she do it? And the answer, of course, is that she doesn't. She pays someone else to do the work of motherhood for her so that she can pursue a career. She can't, after all, be in two places at one time.

Myth #3
Full-time motherhood is boring.

There are many ways to respond to this depiction of full-time motherhood. The first thing that always comes to my mind is what people mean when they use the word *boring*. To suggest something is boring implies that there is not enough work to do to keep oneself busy, and this is hardly the case with motherhood. Indeed, the last thing mothers are is bored. I can just hear my full-time mom friends now, "I would love to be bored! Bored sounds fabulous!" On the other hand, if a person is referring to the work itself as being boring, that's something else. It's true that taking care of children all day is not the most exciting job in the world. But focusing on this fact is a mistake because it will lead us to overlook what we gain and, more important, what our children gain.

We discuss, for example, how hard it is to read the same book over and over again, or how boring it can be to watch *Sesame Street* with one's children or take them to the park for the umpteenth time. But the point is not whether this is true—as raising children does have moments of boredom—the point is that, while we may not find these mundane events exciting, children do.

Children *do*.

Furthermore, this "boredom" women refer to is fleeting and will never eradicate the overwhelming joy that children bring. After all, no job is perfect. There will always be something missing from every job we pursue; there is no way to be completely fulfilled all the time.

A career may seem more exciting when we're pushing our children on the swing on a Wednesday morning—and it may be. But it will never compare.

There are reasons that today's women refer to being at home as boring (a term, by the way, that was never used in previous generations). For one thing, adults now move at lightning speed, so the idea of having to move slowly—as all children do—is challenging. (I discuss this further in chapter five.) Boring, to us, means a lack of stimulation. If we're not constantly running somewhere, we don't know what to do with ourselves. This is unfortunate, for motherhood is a true opportunity—perhaps the only opportunity—to stop the rat race and explore our many other talents. At what other point in your life do you have the freedom and flexibility to be your own boss? Full-time motherhood offers women complete control of their lives, and it's up to us to learn how to use it.

Second, our generation does not embrace sacrifice. The practice of doing for others, of finding personal satisfaction in helping others, is foreign to us. We have been taught that immediate gratification—whether in the form of a paycheck, a pat on the back, or the ability to do what we want, when we want—is the only way to be happy. But as Sir Wilfred Grenfell once said, "Real joy comes not from ease or riches or from the praise of men, but from doing something worthwhile."[14]

The third reason today's women refer to full-time motherhood as being boring is precisely because too many mothers have left home for the workplace. Had they not, full-time motherhood would not be boring—because women would have other women with whom to share the experience! It's adult contact that mothers want; and when mothers used to have it, no one ever thought of motherhood as boring.

Finally, there is a secret that lies buried beneath all the motherhood rhetoric: Children are fun. Unless you're a snob, or one of those people who has no desire to communicate with children on their level (in which case you might think twice before having children in the first place), you may just find that children are more fun than many of the adults you know. "Indeed, the dark secret of [motherhood]—the thing that none of us knew until we gave up our paid jobs—is that it's fun. And deeply gratifying," writes Gurdon.[15]

Myth #4
Full-time motherhood propels a woman into domesticity.

Well, yes and no. A lot has happened since the days when mothers were scrubbing kitchen floors and making homemade bread. We live in a time when technology continues to change things on the home front. Women no longer slave away in the kitchen, and ironing is all but forgotten. Just about the only thing women—and men—have to do to keep house today is know how to work a microwave and push a vacuum.

There's no question we've come a long way. In April 2002, PBS aired a series called *Frontier House*, which depicted family frontier life in 1883. Three modern-day families volunteered to live in Montana for five months, replicating life just as it was in 1883. It was fascinating. As I sat glued to my chair for three consecutive evenings, two hours at a time, I thought about how impossible it is for any of us to grasp what women of that time had to endure. The typical mother in those days would raise her children while doing grueling work. She would start the stove each morning and tend it throughout the day. She would walk miles to get water. And she would prepare three meals a day using only the most basic ingredients and equipment. This only scratches the surface, of course, but the point is this: we are so far removed from such a life that we've become utterly immune to even the idea of hard work. True, this kind of life existed many years ago, so long ago it hardly seems relevant. But is it? For while it may be a bit too much to expect us to appreciate the water we come by so easily, is it too much to expect that we should clean our homes, throw dirty clothes in the washer and dryer, prepare three meals a day, and put dishes in the sink without complaining? I don't think so. We are, in fact, the luckiest women in the world. The kind of labor women used to do—even our own grandmothers and mothers—is utterly foreign to us. I can't help thinking about how any woman over sixty years old must look at our lives and think we're the most spoiled generation they've ever seen.

Which, of course, we are. After all, life at home can't get any easier. There should be little left to complain about.

Myth #5
Motherhood doesn't have to mean sacrifice.

For the past several years, there has been a great deal of material written by women regarding the idea of maternal sacrifice. Some writers suggest that society believes "the good mother" is one who happily sacrifices her entire self for the sake of her family and that any woman who doesn't wish to do this is somehow viewed as less of a mother. As Sylvia Ann Hewlett writes, "If young women are to improve their options and widen their choices, they will need to get over this first hurdle: how to combat the attitude so prevalent in our culture that it is somehow unseemly—or greedy—for a woman to want success in more than one sphere of her life. Somehow a woman isn't a woman unless her life is riddled with sacrifice."[16]

I disagree. At no other time in history has it been more acceptable for women to want the same two things out of life that men do: work and family. In fact, it's not only acceptable for women to want this, it's expected of them. It is now rare to find a woman who doesn't want both work and family in her life. The issue in the working-mother debate is not, as Hewlett suggests, whether women should have interests outside of motherhood, but whether women should make *any* concessions to motherhood. In other words, it's not whether mothers work outside the home at all, it's *how much* and *how often* they think they should be allowed to work outside the home.

The women's movement sold women a bill of goods. Its philosophy states that women are no more inclined toward sacrifice than men are—and that even if they are, they should not be the ones to make the sacrifices involved in motherhood. But this is absurd. Not only are women more naturally giving than men, they are the ones who want to make sacrifices. They are most likely to give of themselves, not because society forces them to, as women's groups like to claim, but because they choose to, because it is natural for them to do so. This is why women have, until recently, been held in higher esteem than men. Moreover, the philosophy suggests that the only way women can achieve happiness is by avoiding the sacrifices of motherhood and focusing instead on self-fulfillment. But what many working mothers still haven't figured out is what some of the greatest philosophers and spiritual leaders of our time have always known: sacrifice is the only path to happiness and self-fulfillment. Doing for others is the only thing in life that can truly feed our souls. When we ignore this fact, we are left with a void.

Any mother who believes she should be exempt from making sacrifices for her children misses the whole purpose of motherhood. It is only by doing the work ourselves—by making the sacrifices—that we grow. As Linda Burton writes, "It seems to me that when we are presented with our greatest opportunity for self-revelation and growth, we are presented with an opportunity to come out on top. We may be frightened of mothering. We may not feel up to it, we may run from its challenges, and we may call our fear a simple born ineptitude for the job. But then we will never experience the sea, and we will never see the view from the mountaintop."[17]

Myth #6
Full-time mothers lose their identities.

Perhaps the greatest myth that the women's movement has perpetuated is the idea that because a mother's work requires her to give so much of herself, it is inevitable that she will lose her identity. "Mothers should work outside the home. Otherwise, they cannot preserve their identities," writes Joan K. Peters in *When Mothers Work: Loving Our Children Without Sacrificing Ourselves.*[18] Women like Peters have been so successful in preaching this theory that women who are not yet mothers presume they will suffer this fate and plan on returning to the workforce after they have children.

The discussion of what happens to a woman's identity when she becomes a mother has become far too myopic. Yes, it is true that once upon a time mothers were not expected to have lives of their own and thus sacrificed everything for the sake of their children. And, yes, it is true that the children of these women, no matter how grateful they were for the sacrifices their mothers made, wanted their mothers to have lives of their own. But the fact remains that we've gone too far in trying to change things. In our attempt to seek identities separate from men and children, women have sacrificed full-time motherhood altogether. Consequently, children have suffered—and so have women, as many have now come to regret the choices they made. Simply put, we have allowed our focus on the Self to cloud our vision of what it means to love others—even, on occasion, at our own expense.

Sacrifice is a reality of life, even for men. While fathers in no way come close to making the sacrifices that mothers do, they are still forced to curtail their own needs in order to address the needs of their families. They may want to play golf every Saturday or go drinking with their buddies every night after work, but they will refrain from doing so if they want a happy family life. (And a mature man would rather spend time with his family anyway.) They may want to quit their jobs, but they do not have this luxury if they expect to feed their families. Being married and having a family is, by definition, a sacrificial role. Thus, it is only natural that the more sacrifices one makes, the more one's identity (even a man's) gets lost in the process.

Most important, however, is what we refuse to see about sacrifice: what we *gain*. Our identities are constantly in flux. Full-time motherhood does not cause a woman to *be* any particular way; it is a woman's personality and attitude that determines her fate as a mother. Every one of us has a choice to look at the glass half empty or half full. Just because women's groups refuse to look at the glass half full doesn't mean we have to follow suit. And just because some full-time mothers—either in the 1950s or today—choose to live their lives through their children, paying little attention to their own needs, does not mean that this is an inevitability of full-time motherhood. It is simply a choice some women make, for whatever reason. Therefore, it makes no sense to say, as Peters does, that all women should become working mothers simply because some full-time mothers are unable to have a conversation about any topic other than their children.

Besides, the reality is that once a woman becomes a mother, her identity does become inextricably linked to her children's. Women simply change when they have children; they are not the same people they once were. Their needs, desires, interests, and world revolves around the needs, desires, and interests of their children, regardless of whether they are with their children throughout the day. "And this is maybe the ultimate irony of her situation: She has gone to work in large part to be free of domestic worries but she is no less consumed by them, even at a distance, encased in her glass tower," writes Danielle Crittenden.[19] The only reason working mothers have instilled the idea that full-time mothers cannot maintain their identities at home is because believing in this myth is the only way they can feel better about their choice not to be home with their children. Deep down, they know they cannot get along without their careers, and they are inherently insecure about their attempt to weave motherhood into their lives. Because the fact is, if a woman *needs* something external—like a career—in order to feel good about herself, then she doesn't have a strong sense of self to begin with. As Maria Shriver writes in *Ten Things*, "Even though you may think your job is your life and your identity, it's not and it shouldn't be."[20] Indeed, a woman's identity should be of her own making, for her strength and power come from within. Being full-time mothers—being "locked in our cages"—shouldn't really matter at all.

Myth #7

A mother who is home with her children wastes her education.

It's a common myth. And perpetuating it—as the character Amy does
on the television show *Judging Amy*, when she suggests to her daughter that her friend's mom stays home with him because "she can't do
anything else"—is the mark of true ignorance. For there is no such
a thing as a woman wasting her education on motherhood. In fact,
quite the opposite is true. Recent studies have shown—as common
sense would conclude—that children who are raised by mothers with
advanced degrees and previous work experience have an advantage
over those whose mothers do not have such backgrounds. If we think
about it, we can see how foolish this myth is. How is it possible that a
woman can *waste her time* raising the next generation, simply because
she's a highly educated individual? Since the work of motherhood is
no different than teaching, wouldn't it make sense that a child is at a
distinct advantage being raised by an educated mother?

And it's not just the children who benefit. The few years we have at
home with our children can be the most educational years of our lives
as well. It's a matter of how you choose to look at it: if you belabor the
fact that the work is monotonous—which it is—and on a level that
is "beneath us" as educated women—which it is not—you will miss
the point. Motherhood is an opportunity to impart our knowledge,
wisdom, and experience to another human being. Children are eager
for everything we have to offer. The better educated we are, the better educated our children will be. Most mothers who return to the
workforce almost always provide their children with less educated
caregivers (with the exception of low-income families): nannies and
day care providers are not positions commonly sought by women with
advanced degrees. Thus, when the educated mother chooses to pursue
a career instead of being home with her children, what she invariably
tells her children is that her education and abilities are so superior that

to stay home to pass this knowledge and intellect on to them would be a waste of time. *– some message!*

⁓

The genesis of these myths lies, of course, in the women's movement, whose founders were among the first to view motherhood in a less than positive light. Over the years, the pressure to conform to feminist ideals—to *believe* what we've been told about motherhood—has become palpable. What many people do not realize, however, is that these myths were created by women who were unhappy in their personal lives. As Betty Friedan writes, "I almost lost my own self-respect trying to hold onto a marriage that was based no longer on love but on dependent hate. It was easier for me to start the women's movement than to change my own personal life."[21] Rather than face her own demons, then, Friedan—like today's working mothers—lashes out at society (men, employers, the government) and blames it for her discontent. And Friedan's ideas have been perpetuated over the years by other unhappy women or women who are simply more interested in women's advancement than they are in children's welfare. But these women do not represent the majority of Americans. The only reason the myths prevail is because they are espoused by some of the most powerful voices in America. They have a vested interest in working motherhood, and their biased view has caused considerable damage to children and families.

Let's begin with gender feminists. This group has not only been vocal in the political arena and in public policy, they have written scores of books and articles that focus on a woman's right to have children without the intention of raising them. Simply put, gender feminists believe that they can love two things equally—their work and their children—and therefore do not think they should have to choose between the two. They feel that being forced to do so would return women to the dark ages, when women had no voice. The most important thing in the world, say gender feminists, is women's rights. Women must be happy, above all else; so if mothers feel they need to be career women, that's fine. Children do not really need their mothers anyway; they can "thrive" in day care, given the right setting. These are women who believe that full-time motherhood is a matter of choice, not responsibility. Betty Holcomb, author of *Not Guilty! The Good News for Working Mothers*, even subtitles one of the chapters in her book "The Myth of Personal Responsibility." Furthermore, say gender feminists, if women feel insecure about their decision to return to the workforce, this has nothing to do with them. The only reason they are hesitant is that husbands and employers are unsupportive of mothers who work. (An absurd claim since today's husbands have no voice if they want their wives to stay home and employers have gone out of their way to support working mothers.) Our society, they say, ostracizes mothers for their career ambitions and expects them instead to be the Perfect Mother. *This* is why mothers feel guilty about leaving their children every day: they're victims.

Susan Chira, working mother and author of *A Mother's Place: Choosing Work and Family Without Guilt or Blame*, took a six-month maternity leave (from her job as deputy foreign editor at the *New York Times*) that she found to be "oppressive" and "boring."[22] She describes her first year of motherhood as being nothing like what some of her friends experienced or what she imagined it to be. In describing the moments with her daughter, she writes, "There were moments of ecstasy: staring at her hands sketching balletic movements in the air; the weight of her soft, warm body when she drifted to sleep on my chest; her first laugh. But I was drowning."[23]

Apparently the sacrifices involved in caring for a newborn got the better of Chira, so back to work she went. But not before writing a book that purports to absolve working mothers of guilt and blame. Rather than admit she couldn't handle the job—which would have been far more admirable—she writes that "sacrifice has no place in the motherhood pantheon,"[24] and then justifies her decision to return to the workforce by creating falsehoods about mothers and children, such as the idea that mothers and children can be apart for hours or days with no ramifications. Or that day care is perfectly fine for children as long as its quality is high. But no matter how many myths women like Chira create to make themselves feel better, what is overwhelmingly obvious is that they return to the workforce for only one reason: It is the easier job.

Which is, of course, the other big secret about why mothers choose to work. A woman I know recently told me that her working mom friends tell her each time they have another baby how they can't wait to get back to work after maternity leave end so they can "have a break." And while it is certainly understandable that a new mother may want nothing more than to run and hide, it is not understandable that she would allow her emotions to drive her out of the house for good. The only conclusion to draw from this is that such women never really wanted to be mothers in the first place. What drives them, perhaps, is the *idea* of being a mother, not actually being one. Perhaps it's the coming home at the end of the day and being lavished with love and attention that really matters to them. The truth is, some women want to have children because they love the idea of being with children, while other women just want children. As one woman tells Peggy Orenstein, "I want to have kids, I just don't want them in my life."[25] Any woman who goes to work by choice clearly feels this same way about children. She just wouldn't dare admit it. But the fact remains that these are women who consider a life at the office to be more enticing than life at home with whiny, food-soaked toddlers.

Sociologist Arlie Hochschild was the first to identify this group of women in her book *The Time Bind: When Work Becomes Home and Home Becomes Work.* Her groundbreaking study revealed the truth about working motherhood: that many women (in all socioeconomic groups) flee the pressures of home for the ease and orderliness of the workplace. One woman tells her, "I always tell people here that I come to work to relax. I know to some people this sounds mean, but to me it's eight hours of relaxation. I can go to work and the kids aren't right in front of me to worry about. At work, I can do more of what I want. At home, I have to do what the kids want."[26] In 1997, an article in *U.S. News and World Report* entitled "Lies Parents Tell Themselves About Why They Work" exposed this truth as well. It outlined the reasons parents give for choosing to work and explained the discrepancies in their claims. The theme of the article is similar to Hochschild's: that despite people's excuses, the truth is that some parents would simply rather be at work. And it is because of this deception that the idea of mothers going to work goes unchallenged. It gives parents permission to avoid the responsibility they have to their children. "The lies parents tell themselves—combined with the fraudulence of the public debate—make it difficult to devise reform or change in attitudes in a way that might ease pressures on families."[27] Indeed, this fraud does a great disservice to women and children, as raising families is no longer considered a parent's obligation but a matter of individual choice. Just as gender feminists always said it should be.

But feminist groups are not as influential as they might hope, at least not in their own right. They have a considerable amount of help from their friends in the media. This is the group with the real power. While journalists cannot say outright—as their gender feminist friends can—that mothers *should* work outside the home, they still manage to convey the message that no woman in her right mind would choose full-time motherhood as a profession.

Gone are television programs and commercials that show mothers at home. Rather than updating programs like *Leave It to Beaver* or *Father Knows Best* with a more realistic depiction of life at home, the folks in television have simply omitted full-time motherhood altogether. Moreover, the news media never discuss or even refer to full-time mothers—as if we have somehow vanished from society. Instead journalists focus on issues related to day care, guilt, stress, and balancing work and family. But the one ramification of working motherhood that the media won't cover is the one that really matters: the children. "The elite journalists in network television don't report the really big story—arguably one of the biggest stories of our time—that this absence of mothers from American homes is without historical precedent, and that millions upon millions of American children have been left to fend for themselves with dire consequences," writes Bernard Goldberg.[28] And the reason the media won't report this story is that, as Goldberg points out in his book, "elite journalists" believe that most Americans think as they do about motherhood. Those in the media do not see their views as liberal at all, he writes, only "sensible, reasonable, rational views."[29] And according to the media, a good and just society would simply accept working mothers.

But being just means being fair, and there is nothing fair about women choosing to have babies only to leave them every day to go do something else. This does not benefit children, families, or society. No one benefits from this choice except perhaps—and of course even this is questionable—women. Clearly, then, tolerance for working mothers is not the mark of a good and just society. It is the mark of a society that plays favorites.

The only way to be truly fair regarding the subject of working motherhood, and thus prove ourselves to be a good and just society, would be to look at the issue holistically, which means studying the negative effects of day care and including in our discussion the voices of full-time mothers, day care workers, and teachers. Unfortunately, we aren't there yet, for America's minority—those powerful voices that emanate from our televisions—are not the reasonable people they think they are. To them, working motherhood can only be discussed in positive terms, which means that information can only be gathered by those who use day care, those who have a vested interest in day care being a good thing. These individuals will rarely discuss the negative aspects of day care because it would mean facing the reality of their own situation.

And so, because the most powerful voices in America refuse to address the real problem of modern-day motherhood, our society never gets to the heart of the matter. Instead, we just dance around it. "Of all the explosive subjects in America today, none is as cordoned off, as surrounded by rhetorical landmines, as the question of whether and just how much children need their parents—especially their mothers. The subject is essentially off-limits for public debate," writes Mary Eberstadt.[30]

The fact is, the most powerful voices in America are not interested in truth at all, and they're certainly not committed to children. The only thing they *are* committed to is "choice"—and, of course, politics. So rather than having an honest and fair public debate about working motherhood, and rather than taking into account the opinion of the real professionals—full-time mothers—they choose to convey the message that not having mothers at home is normal and good, even something to aspire to. They choose to tell America that this trend is here to stay and that balancing work and family is a perfectly workable lifestyle for women. Indeed, just as Friedan wrote that women in the 1950s were defined "solely in terms of their sexual relation to men,"[31] today's women are defined solely in terms of their careers. Children and families come second.

This, say the most powerful voices in America, is progress.

≈

"You're So Lucky You Can Stay Home."

> Many women must work because of material needs,
> but such needs do not begin to account for our
> contemporary rate of maternal absence.
>
> Mary Eberstadt

RARELY WILL A MOTHER ADMIT that she holds on to her career because she feels that without it she has no identity, nor will she admit that society has had any influence on her decision. But then she may not be aware of it. Trends are enormously powerful and sink into our subconscious without our knowledge. Not until years later do we look back and say to ourselves, What was I thinking? It's like fashion. Each decade there is a particular hairstyle or clothing style that is considered "in." We are convinced it looks terrific. But have you ever looked back at, say, the 1980s and seen what we thought looked terrific? It's downright scary.

Cultural trends are not much different. All of us are influenced by what we see and hear around us. This is the reason television is so powerful. The media depend on our being influenced by their messages: this is how they make money. But imagine, for a moment, how you might behave differently—or even *think* differently—if there were no such thing as television. Pretend that you live in the 1920s or 1930s. How do you think your views about motherhood would be different if the only contact you had with the outside world was your family and friends? Just take a moment and think about it: You've never seen television before in your life. Now imagine you are pregnant and about to have a baby. What do you think your natural reaction to motherhood would be? My guess is that unless you were in financial straits, it would not occur to you that you had a choice about whether to raise your child. Now the media is constantly there to remind women that they have a decision to make. "Many women have been seduced by the siren calls of feminist theorizing. Some of us have come to believe that our self-esteem depends upon our jobs and that child care is mind-numbing, spirit-killing drudgery. These are not necessarily statements that women would come up with spontaneously, in the absence of feminist tutoring."[1] The decision to become a "working mother" or a "stay-at-home" mother, then, is a distinct cultural trend. It is the reason every pregnant woman is now asked, "So are you going back to work?"

But those who do decide to go back to work are not comfortable—understandably so—telling people that they work because they want to. So they've come up with a more acceptable reason: money. Never mind that America is wealthier than it has ever been and that today's generation is *the most spoiled generation* in history. This is irrelevant. According to popular belief, most mothers today work because they "have to." In the meantime, the truth—that many women would simply rather be at the office than home with their children—lies buried in our social conscience. Which is why so many working mothers feel a burning need to tell people that they work outside the home for financial reasons. They would rather claim to be among the minority of women who have no real choice in the matter than admit that they just don't want to do the work of motherhood.

This is not to say that all working mothers knowingly misrepresent themselves. Indeed, this is the crux of the problem. There are many mothers who really, honestly believe they have to work. But the reason they do is not that we live in shaky economic times—far from it—but because today's generation has grown up with every possible comfort. They have never faced war or a depression; they have never had to save their pennies and wait until Christmastime to get that one special thing they want; they have never been told they couldn't buy something because they didn't have the cash; they have never been told to walk or ride their bikes somewhere because there was no car available; they have never had to wear the same outfit two days in a row; they have never had to cook from scratch and make do with whatever was in the pantry; and they have never had to clip coupons. Indeed, today's generation has become so accustomed to an easy way of life that they have no idea how to live any other way.

But it's the belief in the idea that most mothers today have to work that has infected society and caused so much damage. For there is now a commonly held belief that women who stay home with their children are among the small, fortunate group of women who are able to do so. It's a working mother's favorite line: "You're so lucky. I wish I could afford to stay home." Today's full-time mothers are constantly being reminded that the only reason they can be home with their children is because they are rich. "The question we ought to be asking is why, in the space of a generation, we have come to consider taking care of our own kids—even if it's just for the few short years before they are in school—as a perk of the rich, like yachting?" writes Danielle Crittenden.[2] Working mothers and child-care advocates have been quick to argue in response that times have changed. In our parents' day, things were more affordable, they say. And yet this argument often "rests on the soaring costs of housing and college tuition, but even those expenses have not risen fast enough to explain the massive entry of women into the work force," write Shannon Brownlee and Matthew Miller.[3] Indeed, the average new home has "38% more square footage than in 1970," so it's not as though we're spending more money than our parents did for the same house. We simply have higher expectations. Take the neighborhood I grew up in, for example. Thirty years ago, the houses were considered sizable (averaging about 2200 square feet), and each house had a good size yard. The neighborhood is also very attractive and in a good location. Today, almost every young couple that has moved into the neighborhood has doubled the size of their home, as families are opting for larger homes and smaller yards. Clearly, what we deem to be affordable isn't what people in previous generations considered affordable. In addition, while the elite private colleges "have soared at nearly twice the rate of inflation in the past two decades, nearly 80% of students attend public colleges, and their average is only $2,800 a year."[4] So the idea that the average family needs to save thousands and thousands of dollars for college is not reasonable. And it's certainly not a reason to become a working mother.

The problem is that we just can't seem to put our wealth into proper perspective. David Brooks talks about "the psychology of abundance" in an article in the *New York Times Magazine*. The abundance of wealth "really does seep into your soul," he writes, causing us to be careless and casual with our money. As a result, "life becomes a vectorial thrust toward perpetual gain and aspiration fulfillment. It takes a force of willpower beyond the call of most ordinary people to renounce all this glorious possibility." This is exactly the reason we refer to full-time mothers as lucky, because the alternative is to believe that these women are somehow able to "renounce" that second income, that they are able to live without abundance. The only reason we choose to view it this way, though, is that Americans have lowered the standard for what constitutes a need. Our "needs" have come to mean six-figure salaries, vacation homes, a third car, and a housekeeper. Anything short of that and we're practically in the poor house. The truth, however, is that we're already rich without these things. As Brooks puts it, "If one's family income is somewhere near the $75,000 mark, "you probably make more than 95% of the people on this planet. You are richer than 99.9% of the human beings who ever lived. You are stinking rich."

Hence, to suggest that full-time mothers are "lucky" is absurd. These women are at home because they would have it no other way, regardless of their financial status. (In fact, most American families in which the mothers are home full-time are *not* wealthy.) Being at home with one's children has little to do with how much money a family makes and everything to do with how people choose to live. Most families in which mothers are home live modestly by today's standards. They do not employ housekeepers, drive fancy cars, go on expensive vacations, or shop indiscriminately. They are families who know how to budget, the way people used to do. Nevertheless, our society readily accepts the notion that it takes two incomes to make ends meet. "It is pathetic that in the year 2001 we have to remind people that two incomes are necessary for basic survival in most families," writes Peggy Orenstein.[5] *Basic survival*? In the twenty-first century? I don't think so.

Few people today—at least those of us born after 1960—have any comprehension of what *basic survival* means. The truth is that middle class working mothers have made money the scapegoat. They have convinced themselves that they have to work because in truth they don't want to—or don't know how to—live on a budget. It makes perfect sense, then, that these women would assume that mothers who are home with their children are "fortunate"—or even rich. Otherwise, why else would they be there? They couldn't possibly *choose* to live on less, so they must be wealthy. "It's easy to get addicted to a certain standard of living, and to make all other lifestyle decisions based on the assumption that both parents have to work full-time," writes Stephen Covey in *The Seven Habits of Highly Effective Families*. "The point is that there are options, there are choices."[6]

Like canceling cable television. Or using cell phones just for emergencies, if at all. Or going out for lunch instead of dinner. Or not going out at all and cooking in your very own kitchen. Or having your husband iron his shirts rather than take them to the dry cleaner. Or making lunch instead of buying it. Or making gifts instead of buying them. (This is a lost art anyway.) Or having dates with your husband that don't require spending a lot of money. Or keeping the same car for ten years. Or using cloth towels instead of paper towels. Or checking books out from the library instead of buying them from a bookstore. (You can even get new releases!) Or not buying your kids a lot of toys they'll never use. Or only going on one vacation every other year. Or living in a smaller home. Or having simple birthday parties at home rather than renting a place. Or only buying clothes you need rather than clothes you want. Or canceling your gym membership and going running instead. Or sharing babysitting duty with your friends rather than paying for a sitter. The point is, if your goal *really* is to be with your children, you will find a way to make it happen. Luck has nothing to do with it. Countless books have been written to help people learn how to live on one income. The information is available for anyone who wants to take advantage of it. Moreover, there has never been a better time to get more for our money. With the fierce competition that exists today, there is no excuse for paying full price for anything. For the first time ever, consumers don't have to sacrifice quality for paying less.

There is no end to the steps a family can take to have a parent at home. Take, for example, those who live in areas such as New York or California where the standard of living really is high, so much so that a person could argue that two incomes are necessary to make ends meet. That this is true does not preclude women from having options. If being home with one's children is a matter of geography, a family can always move. When I was in my mid-twenties and married to my first husband, we lived in the New York area. Although we did not have children yet, I was concerned that the stressful, time-deficient lifestyle, high cost of living, and lack of parental support would not be conducive to a happy family life. He and I did not see eye to eye on this; and though I cannot blame the failure of that marriage solely on this issue, it reared its ugly head on every possible occasion. Needless to say, it is not a coincidence that I now live in the Midwest where things are more affordable and where the quality of life is much better—at least for raising a family. I knew I would miss New York—and I do, very much—I just wasn't willing to compromise when it came to my family. As Covey writes, "The place to start [in seeking a work and family balance] is not with the assumption that work is non-negotiable but with the assumption that *family* is non-negotiable."[7]

Until we are able to do this, we will continue to convince ourselves that most mothers today have to work. And the media must begin to do its part by not supporting the idea that most families today require two incomes to get by and are in desperate need of child care, particularly when there is plenty of research to prove otherwise. As Brownlee and Miller observe, "Better-off Americans are nearly as likely to say they work for basic necessities as those who live near the poverty line."[8] Indeed, if it *were* true that most families could not survive on one income, then why, as we learned in chapter two, do 60.2 percent of married-couples with children below age eighteen have either a non-employed mother or a mother who works only part-time? Clearly, then, the issue is not whether we can afford to be home with our kids, but whether we choose to afford it.

Moreover, it is interesting that those who work solely to make ends meet have no problem admitting that having a mother at home is best, while those who work by choice do everything in their power to dispute this. Mothers who want to be home with their children but cannot be are not the women who tout the benefits of day care or suggest that their children are better off with someone else during the day. It is only the mothers who work by choice that feel the need to tell people that their children are thriving in day care or that they wish they could afford to be home with their children. These women create a litany of rationalizations for why they are working mothers. And for good reason. As Midge Decter writes, "Those who work, not from stark necessity but out of the need in some fashion to make their way in the world, suffer from the pinch of insecurity about the effect on their children of the choice they have made. Such is the inevitable price of worldly ambition."[9]

The assumption that it takes two incomes for most families to make ends meet suggests that having two incomes is always advantageous. In truth, however, many families have found that a second income is no advantage at all. In fact, it can actually *cost* money to work. The money from a second income—unless it's a six figure salary—will be eaten up by commuting costs, child care, eating out, work attire, dry cleaning, convenience foods, and, of course, taxes. By the time you add all that up, there isn't much left. Indeed, the Census Bureau reported in 1997 that the *difference* in the median income level of married-couple families with children below the age of eighteen in which both the husband and wife work "year-round and full-time" and families in which only the husband worked was $17,638. Subtracting work-related costs, you will find that the average two-income family nets perhaps several thousand dollars a year, to say nothing of the cost of time (the focus of the next chapter), which is immeasurable. There is little net gain to a second income.

Not that if there were a net gain—even a clear net gain—it would be a reason to leave our children behind. It is unfortunate, to be sure, that employers dangle money in front of new mothers to get them to stay with their companies, but it is even more unfortunate that new mothers allow themselves to be swayed. It must be difficult, I admit, to walk away from such promises; but once the excitement of money wears off, and women are alone in their homes with their new babies, the decision should seem simple. Indeed, can there really be a price tag on family? Or is it simply a matter of influence? It seems to me that those who are able to walk away from the lure of big money and put their children first will be the most likely to have few regrets—and will be more happy and fulfilled. Most full-time mothers are well aware that if they worked outside the home they could afford a housekeeper or shop whenever they wanted or use babysitters more often. But they also know that these things pale in comparison to being home with their children. They accept that living on a budget is a simple fact of life. For some women (and men), the idea of scaling back or doing without is unthinkable, so they convince themselves that a second income is necessary for their children's happiness and well-being. But the truth is, young children (pre-teens and older notwithstanding) couldn't care less whether they live in a box or a mansion, whether their toys were made or purchased, or whether their clothes are from Target or The Gap. All they care about is whether their parents think they're worth their time.

It's amazing, when you think about it, how much value we place on money. I am reminded of an interview of Matt Lauer of the *Today* show with the actress Julianna Margulies, of *ER* fame. Lauer asked Margulies about her decision to leave the show, and she said that she had done all she could do with the character and that it was time for her to move on. Lauer then mentioned that the show had offered her some "ridiculous sum of money" to stay and wanted to know how she could possibly walk away from that kind of money. Margulies smiled and explained that she had already made a great deal of money and that there were other projects she wanted to pursue. But Lauer wasn't satisfied. He looked at her as though she were crazy. How can you not stay just *one more year* so you can get that salary, he asked. Margulies was forced to repeat her answer. We have come so far that we cannot appreciate why a person would walk away from even more millions of dollars than she already has.

Money is a scary thing. That's why I would never want to win the lottery. Really. It's not that I don't like money; I do. It's just that it holds such *power*. And I truly believe that the only way human beings can stay in control of who we are and what direction our lives will take is if we live, for the most part, on what we need rather than what we want. Indeed, there have been times in my life when money has not been a concern and times when I could barely scrape two dimes together. And I can honestly say that the happiest times of my life had nothing to do with whether I had more than enough money in the bank. I may have been less anxious when I didn't have to worry about money, but I wasn't happier. In fact, money can add to one's problems, for the more money one has, the more money one has to manage. And the more money there is to manage, the more complicated things become. And the more complicated things become, the more potential there is for conflict. Indeed, wealth can cause as much strain in a marriage as can the struggle of never having enough. The truth is that we really don't need as much as we think we do. The only reason we think we do is that people are continuously looking at what their neighbors have. If they could resist this temptation, they might find that they have a great deal more than they think.

None of this is to suggest that one should be happy living on bread and water or that one should never partake of the good things life has to offer. On the contrary, my tastes are as extravagant as the next guy's. The issue isn't that we shouldn't want nice homes or to enjoy living well; it's a matter of being conscious with our spending. There is nothing wrong with being successful or wealthy, but the fact remains that when people have more money than they know what to do with—particularly if they've never known any other way of life—they tend not to appreciate life's small pleasures. Even the big pleasures become no big deal since they can indulge themselves whenever they want. Indeed, one of the reasons wealthy people—*really* wealthy people—are susceptible to discontent or restlessness is because there *is* such a thing as having too much, particularly when it comes at a price. (And the greatest price of all is when mothers choose employment over being with their children.) As the Dalai Lama tells Oprah in the August 2001 edition of *O, The Oprah Magazine*, "When you are discontent, you always want more, more, more. Your desire can never be satisfied."[10] And so it is with money. It has the ability to fulfill our material desires but can deplete us in every other way that matters.

And it has. In Robert Reich's book, *The Future of Success*, he writes that in 1961, 41 percent of college graduates said, more than anything else in the world, they wanted financial success. In 1998, that number jumped to 78 percent. Our desire for success is palpable, and our ambition has paid off: our economy is stronger than it has ever been. But here's the clincher. Reich explains that by becoming wealthier, one would assume we could afford ourselves more time for the more important aspects of our lives, such as our family, friends, and our selves. But, in fact, the opposite has occurred. The wealthier we become, the less time we devote to our lives outside of work. The less time we spend with our families. He writes that the question we should be asking ourselves is, "Would we choose this new reality if we fully appreciated its consequences for the family life we might otherwise have? In other words, is this new economy worth what it costs us?"[11]

One would hope that the answer is a resounding "No." Unfortunately, today's generation sees the world through a very different lens than previous generations. We are by far the most privileged group in history. We travel, shop, eat out, and spend money we don't have. Even the everyday things—DVD, cell phones, Caller ID—do not seem superfluous but necessary—part of our "basic survival." And we had luxuries even before these technological devices. As Anna Quindlen writes in *A Short Guide to a Happy Life* (paralleling Brooks's "psychology of abundance" theory), "Those of us who are 2nd and 3rd and 4th generation are surrounded by nice cars, family rooms, patios, pools—the things our grandparents thought only rich people had. C'mon, let's be honest. We have an embarrassment of riches. Life is good."[12]

Some people believe that, because we have never experienced the financial hardships that people in our parents' generation did, we are somehow better off. But we have only traded one problem for another. Yes, we may be more comfortable than our parents were and struggle less with day-to-day living, but what we have lost is far greater. Because when we are never forced to do without or when we never have to make a choice between two things or when we shop at will regardless of whether we need or can afford something, we lose sight of what really matters. And somewhere, deep down inside, we know this. After all, we inhale books and movies that teach us about the meaning of life, the stories in which a man is lying on his deathbed and his wife sits next to him, realizing that she would trade in all her worldly goods to have him back. It seems that the things we value most in this life are only appreciated after they are taken from us. *This* is why doing without can be so valuable.

Unfortunately, sacrifice and discipline are not qualities that are taught or encouraged in today's society. Take credit cards, for example. They've been around forever, but they've only recently—in the last several decades, that is—been abused. Indeed, the credit card debt of today's average household is $8,367. "Just because I don't have cash for something doesn't mean I shouldn't buy it," says Jen Rinkes, twenty-nine. "I don't think debt is a sin," she adds. "I'm living in a style I want to become accustomed to."[13] Because of this philosophy—the I must have everything I want right this very minute approach—many women are unable to see the big picture of life, particularly when it comes to motherhood. They cannot imagine that the time and effort they would put forth in raising their children is worth more than any amount of money they could ever make. They cannot see that their payment will come much later, after they've done the work. They ignore this bit of wisdom and decide to become working mothers so they can have more money, more things. But what many women still haven't figured out is that less *is* more. A second income may provide their families with more things, yes, but this doesn't necessarily make the family better off. As Gregg Easterbrook points out in his recent book, *The Progress*

Paradox, while the average American's income has doubled in the last fifty years, the percentage of Americans who describe themselves as "happy" is half of what it was. It stands to reason, then, that once we have our basic needs met, having more money often means only having more money to spend. And this has very little to do with improving the quality of family life.

On August 21, 2001, Oprah introduced Ric Edelman, author of *Ordinary People, Extraordinary Wealth*, who explained the difference between wants and needs and proved the concept of "less is more." He said that when people get bogged down with excess, they often get caught up in aspiring for more (as the Dalai Lama said). The only way to gain clarity, then, is to scale down one's lifestyle. Then Oprah introduced Bill and Melissa, a couple that had a great deal of debt. Bill makes $41,000 a year, and Melissa is a full-time mom. In order to get out of debt, they cancelled cable TV, got rid of their cell phone, and began cooking meals at home rather than going out to restaurants. They also used the library rather than purchasing books. The result? They saved at least $6,000. What's more, they found that the time they spent together in the kitchen brought them closer together as a couple. It allowed them to share the household duties, talk with one another, and enjoy a creative process. Bill and Melissa are a textbook example of how less really can be more.

Thomas J. Stanley and William D. Danko discuss this same idea in their book *The Millionaire Next Door*. "Most people have it all wrong about wealth in America. Wealth is not the same as income. If you make a good income and spend it all, you are not getting wealthier. You are just living high. Wealth is what you accumulate, not what you spend."[14] Stanley and Danko should know. They studied the lives of America's most wealthy (defined as people whose net worth exceeds one million dollars) and found that the underlying factor in their wealth was the ability to shun the superficial trappings of a high-consumption lifestyle: expensive clothes, flashy cars, enormous homes, and the like.

Instead, these families—particularly the self-made millionaires—tend to live well below their means. They are people who understand the value of a dollar, often because many of them have lived through hard economic times. To these families, money represents security. Today's generation, on the other hand, hasn't had the "advantage" of living through hard economic times, so money represents something very different: buying power. And therein lies the problem. For once we get a taste of the good life—as people have today—it's almost impossible to go back. As my father used to say, "It's much easier to go up in one's standard of living than it is to go down." This is not rocket science, of course, but the point is well taken. For one of the realities of women's liberation is that couples get used to making a rather hefty income together and having whatever they want, whenever they want. When they are asked to give all that up to raise their children for free, they find that it's just too tall of an order. So they don't give it up.

It is time that we stop making money the scapegoat. Raising children is a choice, not a luxury. Everything we do in life is a choice. "We're always making a choice, although we may prefer to deny that we have choices; we might not want to accept the trade-offs they imply," writes Reich.[15] And except for the very wealthy, the choice to have children will always mean having to give up some things. Maybe even many things. And the fact that our society won't embrace motherhood despite this fact says a lot about who we are. But if there is any ray of light in the dark period surrounding the events of September 11th, it is perhaps a greater appreciation for our values. Even the media changed its tune for a while after September 11th. They discussed whether or not things like money and power still seemed important. "Across every nation, at nearly every level of the workforce, a subtle but far-reaching shift in priorities is under way. Values that were pre-eminent for many people—career, status, money, personal fulfillment—are now taking a back seat to more fundamental human needs: family, friends community, connectedness with others," writes Sue Shellenbarger in the

Wall Street Journal.[16] If this is true, then what we should be seeing is more mothers (or fathers) quitting their jobs and going home to raise their children. Let's hope that they do. Let's hope that women begin to put motherhood into perspective, and that they come to see its value, despite the sacrifice. A former working mother, Linda Burton writes, "Somehow, after the unparalleled experience of knowing children, goals like money and power and prestige have a lot less appeal."[17]

Indeed they do.

~

"I Could Balance Work and Family if I Had More Support."

What kind of example do we set as we race from here to there, trying to accomplish more, have more, experience more? When I am feeling rushed, overworked, and stressed, that quality seeps into the very air around me. In a society that endorses activity, I think we would all do well to put more trust in stillness.

Katrina Kenison

JUST ABOUT THE ONLY TIME it's considered acceptable to spend a lot of time at home is during the holidays. During the holidays, people expect that we'll be holed up in our respites, away from work and all other distractions. We read; we bake; we listen to music; we spend time with our families; we phone our friends and loved ones; we even promise ourselves that we will do more of these things in the New Year. Then the New Year arrives—and we return to the only life we know: work. Not because we prefer it, but because it is familiar. Indeed, work has now become our reason for living, and the home has become almost superfluous.

Admittedly, we cannot blame this new way of life solely on the women's movement. Despite its enormous influence, there is also technology to consider. The advances have been spectacularly successful in steering us away from our homes. The drudgery our ancestors endured is virtually obsolete. Unfortunately, rather than enjoying the time we've gained from our technological advances, we have used it to become twice as productive—when what we should be doing is allowing it to create more free time for us. Because of this, productivity is now the focal point of our lives, while "doing nothing"—even spending time with our kids—is considered a waste of time. "Thirty-eight percent of Americans feel they "waste" their leisure time if they don't accomplish something productive," writes Sue Shellenbarger in *Parade* magazine.[1] And yet it is within this chronic need to be productive that we never really are productive. We spend all our time running from Point A to Point B rather than being successful at any one thing—rather than living life at all.

Indeed, we are virtually handicapped outside of work. We haven't the slightest idea how to be productive, for the moment we do have a minute to ourselves we pick up some technological device, rather than finding our own creative ways to be productive. And in this age of overindulgence, of progress and self-fulfillment, our children have followed our lead. They have become us. As Judith Regan writes in *O*, "'Mommy, I'm bored,' my daughter announces after a day of video arcades, Rollerblading, eating out, and instant messaging her friends. She is, at age 9, bored to death while being bombarded by stimulation."[2] Despite all we have, despite all our supposed advantages, we are discontent, get bored easily, complain about a lack of time, are always in a hurry, and are constantly looking for things to be bigger or better. We have the opportunity to lead more fulfilling lives than previous generations, yes. But we have chosen not to take advantage of it.

Don't get me wrong: I am thrilled to be living in the post-modern era—what with washers and dryers, dishwashers, cordless phones, microwaves, and computers—I'm just not thrilled to be living in a society that has allowed this progress to change who we are. Here again, previous generations were at a distinct advantage. They may have had to wash or make their clothes by hand and live without microwaves, televisions, and computers, but at least they felt a sense of pride and accomplishment for all their hard work. At least they made good use of time. At least they valued their homes and children more than they did their jobs.

Over the last few decades, a great social transformation has taken place in America. Where we once coveted the comfort and security of home and family, as well as honoring the work that went into making a home, we have now turned our attention to the world of work, to paid labor. The psychologist Ilene Philipson writes about this transformation in her book *Married to the Job*, suggesting that we're a nation obsessed with work and that life outside of work has become unfulfilling. She describes the difference between her generation and today's: "Growing up in America after the Second World War, I was part of a social movement that eschewed paid labor and embraced leisure time. Hanging out, that is, unstructured time, time to spend with friends, time to reflect, wonder, and muse, was an overriding goal. Creative work—baking bread, gardening, engaging in traditional forms of art like painting or playing music—and working to make a difference in the world, were highly valued."

Such values are no longer an "overriding goal." The goal now, writes Philipson, is not just to meet our financial needs through work, but our emotional needs as well. Work, not family, is where we find meaning and a sense of accomplishment. Work is where we feel appreciated, where we find our identity. Not surprisingly, however, this goal has failed—for we can never replace what we're missing at home with what we find in the workplace. The workplace is about money and success; family is about human connection, love, and personal growth. And this is where full-time mothers get shortchanged: "We value and admire the adult who spends his or her life living alone, working long hours, more than the individual who cares for others at home."

This was not the case in the past, when "there were means other than work with which to measure oneself as a human being." Today, with all our wealth, we measure our worth according to our ability to work long hours and become wealthy while doing so. Our need to keep up with the Joneses is palpable. Which is why, although technology could afford us more leisure time, we choose instead to live an accelerated lifestyle. "We may very well have an hour more than we did 30 years ago, but we're moving at a much faster pace, which leaves us feeling stressed,"[3] writes Karen Levine in *Parenting* magazine. She adds, "Theoretically, the purpose of leisure time is to offer psychological renewal from work, but when we spend our leisure hours at the same kind of frenetic pace as our work hours, we emerge feeling drained."[4] And it's our choice of activities that work against us. Previous generations would spend their leisure time playing cards and games, or talking, reading, and making scrapbooks for their children. They would put photo albums together, read novels, write letters to their friends, and take long walks. We do none of these things. Just about all of our free time is spent in front of the television or running errands while we talk on our cell phones or shopping for no particular reason, except that we're bored.

You would think we'd have learned our lesson by now. You would think we'd have realized that our incessant need for things to be bigger, better, more doesn't make families stronger. It weakens them. But for some reason, we haven't made this connection. So let me reiterate what should be obvious. Televisions, computers, cell phones, email, beepers, and the Internet keep us from being productive and connected to one another. They keep us from doing things we can feel good about, things like reading, sewing, carpentry, and gardening, things like cooking and cleaning (Yes, cooking and cleaning can actually give you a feeling of self-worth—try it!), things like writing letters or diaries and playing games with our children. These activities allowed previous generations to lead richer, more fulfilling lives. Our idea of a rich and fulfilling life means work and more work. It means running through life, full speed ahead. And we give no thought whatsoever to what gets lost in the process. As Laura Pappano says in an interview about her book *The Connection Gap*, "In spite of our ridiculously full lives, it all doesn't add up to what it's supposed to. We're doing all this stuff, but we're not feeling it; it seems to wash over us."[5] This is why, no matter how hard women try to squeeze children in around their hectic career lives, the result will always be chaos. And in the midst of all the chaos, motherhood, too, washes over us.

Balancing Work and Family

American Heritage's definition of the word "balance" is a state of equilibrium or parity characterized by the cancellation of all forces by equal, opposing forces, and a harmonious or satisfying arrangement or proportion of parts or elements. Since the part of one's life must be proportionate to one another to achieve an harmonious arrangement, it is impossible for working mothers to achieve balance because the amount of time they spend at the office is entirely out of proportion to the time they spend with their children. A working mother's relentless search for balance will be futile. "We can't be fully at home and fully at work at the same time. Work and life don't overlap so much as they collide or intersect, leaving us to sit in our ergonomically correct swivel chairs and pivot between the two. And each time we turn toward one, we are, in that moment, turning away from the other," writes Lisa Belkin in *Life's Work*.[6]

Indeed, not one of the solutions working mothers have come up with over the years has worked. Here is a just a sampling of what the parenting "experts" suggest working mothers do in order to create balance: don't bring your work home with you, even the mental part; have weekly pow-wow sessions with your family to coordinate the week's activities; spend all day Sunday making dinners for the week; set three daily priorities; establish your goals; make time to plan; don't cram on the weekends; or—this one's my favorite—take some time for yourself when you come home before you put on your Mom hat. As if working moms haven't already had a giant break from their kids, as if their kids need to wait any longer for their mothers' attention. But while working mothers try hard to implement these strategies, all they succeed in doing is using up even more time.

Despite all of this, women continue to look for that magical answer, for they would rather bear the stress of trying to balance work and family than admit that it just isn't possible. Meanwhile, the voices of doom are all around them. Maushart writes, "Women who juggle for a living and do it badly—which is to say, most of us—spend so much time chasing dropped balls that they have little energy to observe, let alone to question, the rules of the game."[7] Even an article in *Working Mother* magazine admits that when mothers attempt to balance work and family, it's more likely that their work lives will intrude on their home lives, rather than the other way around. The article refers to a report that was done by the Families and Work Institute: "A demanding job leaves almost half of parents too tired to do things with their children; 60% of working mothers say they have to put work ahead of family at least some of the time; overworked employees feel less successful in relationships with spouses, children, and friends; and they're more likely to lose sleep and feel stress."[8]

Nevertheless, working mothers persevere. And in their search for balance, they may turn to women like Katherine Wyse Goldman, author of *Working Mothers 101: How to Organize Your Life, Your Children, and Your Career to Stop Feeling Guilty and Start Enjoying It All*, who makes a valiant attempt to help women juggle career and family. But her book does nothing of the sort. What it does do, remarkably well actually, is teach women how to do the absolute minimum when it comes to raising children. Moreover, Goldman overlooks the many ironies in her own book. She begins by observing that "No mother has ever regretted on her deathbed that she didn't spend enough time at the office," but spends the rest of the book telling women how they can organize their lives and farm out their family responsibilities so that they *can* spend the majority of their time at the office. She does, however, acknowledge that being able to get one's children out of the house in the morning and pick them up at day care really isn't that hard. What's hard, she says, is "that other part of being a mother: turning your innocent, guileless, perfect baby into an adult who's caring, compassionate, sensible, and responsible."[9] This last part is exactly what being a full-time mother is about, but if you are not home to do this work, then turning one's baby into a "caring, sensitive, compassionate, sensible, and responsible adult" will be difficult, if not impossible.

Goldman goes on to admit that she and other working mothers "have to rely a lot on others to know what is going on" with their children and that they "feel terribly guilty that we're not around all the time to guide our children through the minefield of life."[10] She adds, "We work hard, we work late, and we're distracted. As much as we want to think of nothing but our children when we're home, thoughts of impending deadlines creep into our thoughts."[11] Her solution, of course, is to capture quality moments with your children. Take a few moments to lie down with them at night before they go to sleep, she says. Noting that day care workers have said that children of working mothers always seem tired (I discuss this in the next chapter), she responds, "Big deal."[12]

But perhaps Goldman is a bit extreme even for working mothers. In that case, they could always turn to people whose opinions do not stem from defensiveness or justification, but an honest, fair assessment of today's lifestyle. People like Oprah. In her magazine, she talks about the inevitable results of our fast-paced society. "The divorce rate is soaring, parents are spending fewer minutes a day with their children, and friends have to squeeze one another in to their breakneck schedules. As our lives get busier and we move faster, many of us are too exhausted to even enjoy physical intimacy," she writes.[13] Oprah's magazine is the number one magazine in the country, so obviously mothers are reading her words, and yet they are unable to connect the dots between

Oprah's observation and their choice to "have it all." Working mothers just can't accept that their lifestyle causes a ripple effect, as each part of their lives spills over into the other and creates disaster. They just can't see that trying to perform two full-time jobs results only in a time deficit and that no amount of organization is going to change this fact. As Ann Crittenden writes, "Time-use surveys confirm that as women enter the workplace, they take on the equivalent of two full-time jobs, forcing them to cut back on everything in their lives but paid work and children."[14] And yet it is this other part of our lives—these things we're cutting back on—that allow us to lead happy, healthy lives. Just having them back is worth giving up a paycheck.

Errands and Household Chores

Perhaps the greatest fallout of a mother's choice to work outside the home is what happens to her evenings and weekends, coveted time that used to be reserved for spouses, children, and the self. This time is now filled with an endless array of errands and household chores. Feminist groups will claim that the reason for this is because women are still expected to do the lion's share of the household labor and child care. As Betty Freidan writes in the re-released *The Feminine Mystique*, "As we approach a new century—and a new millennium—it's the men who have to break through to a new way of thinking about themselves and society."[15] She says this despite having admitted, several pages earlier, that the latest figures reveal that American men "are now doing 40% of the housework and child care."[16] But that's not good enough, she says. "Men are not yet taking absolutely equal responsibility for children and home."[17] (We must get that extra 10 percent in there.)

Unless you've married a neanderthal, equality has very little to do with what happens to the nights and weekends of a dual-income family. The reason for the ripple effect is time. "The battles [between husbands and wives] aren't always waged over actual chores or the inequity of handling them. The battle is over time," writes Rhonda Nordin in *After the Baby*.[18] If two people are trying to raise children, bring home a paycheck, take out the trash, pay the bills, mow the lawn, paint the shutters, fix the leaky faucet, cook the meals, clean the dishes, go to Target, do the laundry, pick up the dry cleaning, go to Home Depot, shop for clothes, go to the doctor, return phone calls, do the grocery shopping, and go to the gym, they are going to be in overload. No matter how well a mother and father plan this time, no matter who's supposed to be in charge of what, it never runs smoothly. One person always ends up doing more than the other. The only way to end the madness would be for one parent to be exempt from having to produce an income and instead be responsible for raising the children and doing the work of life. And no, this does not mean that men are exempt from household chores and child care in exchange for this setup, because housework and child care, unlike employment, does not have a start and finish time. The work is neverending, and it's too much for one person to do alone.

Leisure Time

Because evenings and weekends are now spent on the household chores and errands that can't get done during the week, we lose all our leisure time. And leisure is what makes our lives meaningful. Today's parents are too busy checking off the next item on their to-do lists to engage in leisurely activities. "Most of us spend our weekends plowing through lists of things we need to accomplish before Monday," writes Karen Levine in *Parents*.[19] Indeed, by the time the clock strikes five on a Saturday, it's as though we've had another day at work.

But the most significant outcome of the ripple effect, specifically as it pertains to household chores and leisure time, is that women have lost something extremely valuable, more valuable than they realize. In our obsession with living a fast-paced life—in which more work means more money, which means more pleasure—we have overlooked those everyday things that can nourish our souls, because invariably this lack of time forces us to pay others to do our work for us. "When we delegate too readily we diminish something that, as a society, we are let slipping away: a sense of competence. When you do something yourself, especially when you do it well, the silent companion to the accomplished job is the knowledge of your own ability," writes Pappano.[20] She adds that it has been "fashionable to joke about our ineptitude" for performing routine household chores and engaging in such pastimes as sewing and cooking.[21] (I am reminded of female morning news anchors who, when they stand beside chefs as they demonstrate to the audience how to prepare certain foods, are quick to point out in a sardonic tone that they have no ability or time to cook.) As one woman who "has made a business of tending to other people's lives," helping families do everything from finding their keys to packing their kids' school lunches, tells Pappano, "If you don't put the work into something, you don't know the worth of it."[22]

The same holds true for raising children. If you pay someone else to do the work for you, you can never appreciate it.

Friendships

Friendships are highly underrated, and we have compromised them as well. We say that we want more time for our friends, yet we continue to live our lives in a way that leaves no room for them. If we truly understood that friendships are critical to our mental health—particularly for women—then we would leave some room for them to flourish. And the only way mothers can do this is if they are home full-time. "Overwhelmed by the demands on our time, energy, and emotions, it's easy for us working moms to blow off our friends,"[23] writes Betsy Currier Beacom. She adds, "One of the biggest culprits is time. There simply aren't enough hours in the day. This is where at-home moms have the advantage: They often bump into other moms at the playground and follow up with lunch and an extended playdate, or stay for a chat after the school pick up."[24]

This lack of friendships is yet another consequence of working motherhood, and it is unfortunate that working mothers do not see their value. Not only are friendships fun (Are we allowed to have fun anymore?), they are vital to our mental health. I am fortunate to be blessed with great friends, and as a full-time mom, I am utterly dependent on them. Indeed, the fact that so many mothers now return to the workforce is the reason many women feel isolated when they are home with their children. Women of the past didn't have these concerns. Mothers were everywhere; neighborhoods were filled with life; friends were easy to find. This is no longer the case, which is why the average new mother today thinks she has to return to the workforce to find some adult interaction. But the truth is, we full-time moms are everywhere. (Remember, we're the majority, not the minority.) We just have to look a bit harder to find one another.

Less Is More

The ripple effect proves how much more there is to life outside of paid employment. Unfortunately, we have chosen to value money over everything else. We haven't been able to see that it is time that gives life meaning. The more time we have, the better our quality of life is. Any working mother can attest that it is a constant battle to find time. As Orenstein writes about one of the working mothers she interviewed for her book, "Time has been the biggest trade-off in the balance [Emily] has struck between family life and work. Time alone, time with Dan, time with friends, and particularly, time with the children."[25] Amy, a working mother of two, tells Familyeducation.com, "I'm either working or with my kids. I've decided not to do things for myself, like work out, read a book, or spend time with my friends. There's no 'me time.'

You're 'on' at the office, you're 'on' at home. I know intellectually I need to create that balance, but it never happens."[26]

As a mom and a writer, I can relate. Despite being in a highly desirable situation—I work for myself, from home, and mostly during "off hours"—even I do not escape the fallout. In my case, there were three areas I did not allow to be neglected—or even compromised—in my choice to write this book. The first was my daughter; the second was my sleep; and the third was exercise. I told myself that as long as I made these three areas my top priority, then I could handle other areas of my life taking a back seat for a while. The areas I neglected were household chores, leisure time, and my marriage. The moment my daughter went down for her nap (which lasted about two and a half hours) and the moment she went down for the night (about 7:30 PM), I went to work. I did not watch television; I did not read for pleasure; I did not clean the house; I did not answer the phone; I did not talk to my husband; and I prepared the simplest meals I could. I did manage to go out every so often on Friday and Saturday nights, which was a good thing, because those were the times my husband and I actually spent time together. But suffice it to say, I was very glad to have the book finished. After all, what's the point of being married if you never spend any time with your spouse? What's the point of having a kitchen if you're never going to cook? What's the point of owning a home if you're not going to take care of it? What's the point of having friends if you never talk to them? (What's the point of having children if you're not going to raise them?)

The problem is that time is an intangible, so we tend to dismiss it. We prefer to think of time as an hour here, an hour there, but rarely do we consider the emotional spillover that takes place. "Even if there's physical time for friends, family, community, and personal reflection, there's no psychic space left," writes Robert Reich.[27] And this is perhaps the most significant effect of working motherhood that Americans have overlooked. For it is time, not money, that we need more of. Of course, working mothers insist that the answer to their dilemma is organization, or the ability to carve out family time. Goldman suggests, "Don't make plans with other couples on Saturday night. Stay home and make dinner with the family."[28] (There goes your weekend entertainment with other couples.) Or "try to have dinner as a family, even if the children have to wait for you to get home."[29] (Now your kids are cranky because they're hungry.) Or "make plans for one day each weekend."[30] (How will the errands and chores get done?) Such suggestions merely result in stealing time away from other things. As Arlie Hochschild observes, "Paradoxically, what may seem to harried working parents like a solution to their time bind—efficiency and time segmentation—can later feel like a problem in itself."[31] Indeed, moving faster in order to create quality time does not result in quality time at all because quality time ends up taking a "special discipline, focus, and energy, just like work."[32] Moreover, women discover that wrench after wrench is thrown into their plans because they did not anticipate the general spontaneity of life, what they didn't plan for but which nevertheless came up.

Working mothers just don't get it. There *is* no time. The only way to find time is to quit their jobs. The less we do, the more time we have. The more time we have, the more connected we feel. The more connected we feel, the happier we are.

Less is more.

Unfortunately, logic is not part of the philosophy of working mothers. Of course they could juggle two full-time jobs, they say, if they only had the support they needed from society. Peggy Orenstein asserts that "maybe it's not mothers' withdrawal from the workplace that's called for but support, appreciation, and reassurance—from employers, friends, family, and in particular, husbands."[33] But employers, friends, family, and husbands have been nothing but supportive. Indeed, there has never been a better time in history for mothers to be supported in their choice to work outside the home. Most companies are as family-friendly as they possibly can be. Even *Working Mother* admits that it's "unrealistic to expect any company to meet all its employees' child-care needs."[34] Moreover, today's husbands are not only more involved at home than they ever have been, but they fully support their wives' choice to work, even if they don't agree with it. When was the last time you heard the husband of a working mother tell you that he would prefer it if his wife would stay home and raise their children? He'd rather stick a needle in his eye than say such a thing. The reason the work and family balance continues to be elusive is not the insensitivity of men and employers, but that raising children has always been, and will continue to be, a full-time job. And no one, male or female, can successfully perform two full-time jobs at the same time. Period.

In fact, this has been true since women first attempted the juggling act. In the 1960s, my own mother tried to combine a career as a stockbroker with motherhood. Despite having an ideal setup—a nanny-housekeeper and a job two minutes from home—her balancing act lasted less than five years. She thought it was working well when she had only one child, but after she had a second child, everything changed. There was simply no time, energy, or ability to do it all. And to this day, as my mother watches me spend my days focused on my work as a mother, she regrets having missed those first few years at home with my sister and me.

Balance was still elusive in 1989, when Hochschild interviewed Ann Myerson, a working mother of two, for her book *The Second Shift*. Myerson told Hochschild that she tried all the strategies to create balance: she kept her children up at night to spend "quality time" with them; she farmed out most of her household duties to her children's nanny; she left her work—both physically and mentally—at the office; and she cut back on spending time with friends. But nothing worked: "I don't like what's going on at home. My husband is terrific. I've had all the help money could buy. I've had a fifteen-minute commute, and it still hasn't worked out."[35] So she quit.

And now, here we are fourteen years later. As one woman describes her former life as a working mother to Nordin and Gjerdingen, "I got the baby ready for day care, dropped her off, and picked her up each day after work. Then I fixed dinner, cleaned up the kitchen, bathed the baby, put her to bed, and with whatever energy I had left, picked up the debris left around the rest of the house. On weekends, I ran errands, picked up groceries, really cleaned the house, did laundry—and, oh yes, spent "quality time" with the baby. I lost all track of family and friends, dropped all volunteer activities, and gained 10 lbs. Bedtime became my opiate. And, of course, I didn't feel like making love. I was exhausted."[36]

It is abundantly clear that over the course of their now thirty-year search for balance, working mothers have come up empty-handed. They're still searching, of course—they probably always will—but no matter how hard they try, they will never succeed. For if the goal of balance is to enjoy our work, our selves, our marriages, and our children, then full-time motherhood is the only way to achieve such balance. Full-time motherhood alleviates most of the stress that we associate with today's "working" families: work pressures, traffic and long commutes, and an incessant time deficit. The beauty of full-time motherhood is that, although it is a 24-7 job, it has enormous flexibility. Indeed, one of the best things about full-time motherhood is that women are not in a rush. Whatever they can't accomplish one day, they can always accomplish the next. Furthermore, there are no dead-lines; and there is no one to answer to. This alone is worth giving up a paycheck. As Jill Larson, a woman who left an executive-level job to be a full-time mom, states, "Please don't complain to me about how stay-at-homes don't have balance. I can't tell you how many moms with kids I see sitting around having coffee at Starbucks every time I'm there. I'm actually able to work out again at our local YMCA . . . Would I ever had had the time to do that before when I was working? Never. Having been on both 'sides,' I'd say the stay-at-homes have it pretty good."[37]

The Truth about Guilt and Stress

Guilt used to be a relatively simple concept. If you did something wrong, you knew it. Your conscience would tug at you, and you would feel bad. And you would continue to feel bad until you rectified the situation. When it comes to motherhood, however, guilt becomes a bit more complicated. There are two kinds of guilt mothers feel. There's real guilt, the kind that eats away at you because you know you've done something wrong and your conscience is not letting you off the hook; and there's unfounded guilt, the kind that rears its ugly head at a mother's slightest misstep but is, for the most part, fleeting and irrational. Maria Shriver acknowledges these two aspects of guilt in her book, *Ten Things*. She defines guilt as her "gut talking to me."[38] She says that as a working mother she felt guilty all the time and was very concerned that her children might think Boris Yeltsin was more important to her than they were. Now that she's a full-time mom (and the first lady of California), she says that her children joke with her by telling her she's not around enough. "But the difference is," she says, "I let it roll off my back, because I know it's not true. If it were true, the guilt would be intolerable."[39] It is only natural that mothers want to do right by their children and therefore tend to fear that any slip will cause irreparable harm. Such feelings are normal, even good. But working mothers have distorted this reality to suggest that women should be able to have children without the intention of raising them and not feel bad about it. And that's a whole different kind of guilt.

For example, if I get a babysitter for a few hours one week so that I can go shopping or go out with my friends in the evening, or if my husband and I want to use a sitter on a Friday or Saturday night, I think nothing of it because I have the advantage of knowing that my daughter has my undivided attention, just as she's entitled to, for the majority of my waking hours. Now, if I were away from my daughter all day, every day, while someone else did the work of motherhood for me, you can bet I would feel guilty. Because if I chose to be away from my daughter in order to fulfill my career needs, I would have no business spending even more time away from her. My conscience would always be there to remind me.

There's no way to feel serious, debilitating guilt if there is nothing to feel guilty about. A woman who cannot rid herself of guilt, whose heart feels as though it is being crushed, has simply made a bad decision. This is the nature of guilt, and it is the same guilt that all mothers feel when they choose to place their children in someone else's care. The only reason the definition of guilt has become so skewed is because women try to find a way to avoid their guilt, justify their guilt, or blame their guilt on others. Susan Chira argues that working mothers would not feel guilty if they lived in a society that encouraged them to be proud of their choice to work outside the home: "One weekend morning, when I was too exhausted to even play with my children, I struggled to hold back tears, lashing myself with the same accusations that enraged me when others leveled them at working mothers."[40] No mother would "lash herself" because of what others think about her lifestyle unless she herself feels ambivalent about it. Women who work out of necessity, those who leave their homes every day in order to put food on the table but who would much rather be home with their children, would never find themselves in Chira's shoes—"lashing themselves"—because they know they have no choice. They may feel a sense of guilt because their children are getting second best, but they are never forced to wonder whether they're doing the right thing because they know their children would otherwise not have the most basic necessities. The same holds true for a single mother, who may feel badly about her children having to suffer because they do not have a father in the home. She will not suffer genuine guilt because she knows she has no choice but to work. Thus, mothers who work out of true necessity do not suffer the same guilt as mothers who choose to work, because mothers who have to work *are not making a choice at all.* Those who work by choice, on the other hand, are in a constant battle with their consciences. As Judy Chicago, a former feminist, tells Smith College graduates, "If you choose to raise children, your careers will suffer; and if you choose careers, your kids will suffer—and so will you from the guilt and compromises you'll be forced to make." [41]

A working mother's guilt can be seen on many different levels. The most common source of guilt comes from the lack of time she spends with her children. A working mother is acutely aware of how much attention her children have had—or, more likely, have not had—from her on any given day. Thus, in trying to enjoy the simple pleasures she is entitled to—a long bath, a date with her husband, a weekend afternoon to herself—she is hit with a wave of guilt. How can I get a babysitter and go out at night when my children haven't seen me all day? How can I steal a few hours to myself when my children never get to see me? And more often than not, she will give these things up. (And this is what leads to her unhappiness.) But nowhere is a mother's guilt more palpable than when she decides to place her baby in day care. "It was really hard for me. I cried. It took me two weeks to realize I wasn't harming him. I felt so guilty," writes Donna Perlowski, a Dallas mother, when she first took her son to day care. [42] Perlowski is not alone. Most working mothers are wracked with guilt when they first take their babies to day care. Indeed, I would be concerned about any mother who is not wracked with guilt and anxiety upon dropping off her six-week old baby in the care of strangers all day, every day. The question we should be asking is: What separates the mothers who learn from their guilt and quit their jobs, from those who "work through their guilt," until it eventually subsides?

It has been said that some mothers just don't care, and perhaps there is some truth to this. But I don't think that's the main reason. I think the main reason is that the message these mothers receive from society is that working motherhood is a natural, normal thing. It is, after all, abundantly clear from the research is that the overwhelming majority of working mothers do feel guilty about working outside the home, which does not indicate a lack of concern on their part. The problem arises when they seek advice about the source of their guilt. Over and over again, they are told that their guilt has nothing to do with their consciences trying to tell them something, but that society has imposed this guilt upon them. Thus, the mother who teeters fragilely on the precipice of guilt is immediately exonerated. So back to work she goes. And the next time her conscience begins to nudge her, or the next time she sees something in her child that she believes may have to do with her absence, she reminds herself that these feelings have nothing to do with her. It's society's fault that she feels the way she does. Moreover, women like Goldman will assure her that this guilty phase will pass. In a chapter devoted to child care, Goldman writes, "Welcome to the top of the guilt list. You could spend months and years feeling terrible about leaving a tiny, adorable infant who has yet to sit up, much less take a step or say 'Mama,' but a better tactic is to dry your tears and suck it up." [43]

Suck it up.

So women give it a valiant effort. They leave the day care center and head to the office to try to focus on work. And soon they are consumed with thoughts of their babies. They miss them; they worry about them; and in the back of their minds there is a gnawing sense of guilt. They find themselves unable to concentrate on their jobs. But, again, no worry: "When you're at work, be there to contribute. When you're tempted to pick up the phone to check on the baby, you learn what guilt is all about. Train yourself to turn it off," writes Goldman. [44]

Turn it off.

So women give it yet another try. And several months or years later, when they realize that their jobs keep interfering with motherhood, they begin to overcompensate for their absence from home. Some pull out all the stops for their children's birthday parties, thinking that an elaborate event will somehow make their children forgive them for being gone all the time. Or they buy their children gifts for no particular reason. And just when they think they have suppressed the guilt, it resurfaces in some other way. When all is said and done, working mothers find themselves in a constant battle with their consciences that is evident every time they talk about their lives. Indeed, have a conversation with the average working mother and you will soon discover that much of it is devoted to her explanation of why she has chosen to work outside the home—a conversation, by the way, that never takes place with mothers who have no choice but to work. And because there are so many women in this situation, working mothers feel vindicated as they painstakingly make their way through the maze of guilt.

Stress is the other favorite topic among working mothers. The media love to talk about stress as though it were an everyday thing for the majority of Americans. As usual, they seek "experts" who make suggestions as to how people—women in particular—can relieve their stress. Sue Shellenbarger's article in *Parade* magazine, which discussed the balancing act of a typical two-income family, was refreshingly candid: "The couple rose at 5:00 AM, rushed through breakfast, raced to drop their daughter at day care, commuted thirty miles in opposite directions to demanding jobs, and raced back to pick up Muriel."[45] Mary, the mother, tells Shellenbarger that she and her husband didn't have time for each other and that whatever time they did have was spent on household chores. She said that the strain was affecting their marriage and that their daughter was showing signs of anxiety. "The way we were living had to change," says Mary. When they realized their priorities had "gone awry," the answer seemed obvious: Richard, the father, quit his job.[46]

While such stories aren't rare, we rarely hear about them. We have to come to this realization on our own, because society is not going to help us figure it out. The media will continue to dance around the issue because it is the politically correct thing to do. Indeed, it almost seems as though being stressed out has become a desirable trait. For as much as we may complain, having too much to do makes us feel important. Philipson writes about an occasion in which she and her co-workers were trying to find a mutually desirable time to meet once a month. As they perused their date books to look for possible dates, they realized they could not find a time to meet. Philipson noticed, much to her dismay, that everyone in the group "seemed proud of their overburdened schedules. Suddenly we seemed to be engaged in one-upmanship."

Sadly, women's endless search for balance has all been for naught. More important, it has come at the expense of children and families. Women must begin to accept that there is no such thing as having it all at the same time. We are not more fulfilled as a result of working motherhood. If anything, we are less fulfilled. Although women know that time is their biggest obstacle, they are convinced they can somehow create time. They hold on to the idea that if they could just be better organized, they could create enough time in the day to be successful at both career and motherhood. But there is nothing that any one of us can do about the twenty-four hour cycle; it is here to stay. The only way a working mother can make time is to quit her job. For if we really want to be happy, if saying that we want to get off the treadmill isn't just rhetoric, then we must stop analyzing life's design and get on with the business of living.

We must get on with the business of raising our children.

⤻

"I'm a Better Mom for Working."

Children flourish when they are unhurried.

Inda Schaenen

I F YOU HAVE EVER WALKED ALONGSIDE A CHILD—or bathed, dressed, or fed a child—then you know how slow children are. It begins at birth and continues all the way through adolescence, as parents anxiously tap their feet while waiting for their teenage children to gather their belongings for school. Children, by their very nature, move like snails. We, unfortunately, do not. Ever since work became our priority and technology accelerated our lives, we've been busy, active, on the go. I guess we thought children would adjust.

We thought wrong.

Society may change, but children don't. Each of their activities—walking, dressing, eating, bathing, playing, talking, learning—is very slow. Previous generations understood this and adapted their lives to accommodate the needs of children. (This was, admittedly, easier for them to do since they lived slower-paced lives.) But today we expect children to adapt to their parents' needs. If things don't move quickly enough for us—and children certainly don't—then we can't be bothered. Indeed, our accelerated lifestyle controls us, so much that we don't even think we have a choice to slow down.

We really believe that.

So we've come up with a new way to raise children. We begin by removing babies from their cribs every morning while they are still asleep so we can get them to day care in time for work. We shuffle older children around from home to school to activity as though they are in our way and we need a place to put them. We no longer feed children three healthy meals a day because it takes us too much time to prepare them and children too long to eat them. Finally, we no longer talk to our children—really talk—because we're just too tired to give them our full attention. And still we wrinkle our eyebrows and wonder what's wrong with children today: Why are they not doing well in school? Why are they overweight? Why are they getting into so much trouble? Why are they sleep deprived? Why are they on Ritalin? Why are they so disrespectful? Why are they having so much sex? Why are they spoiled? We simply refuse to see the connection between the problems that exist among today's children and the fact that mothers aren't at home. Just what did we think mothers were for?

Not mothering, that's for sure. I remember combing through an issue of *Parenting* magazine and stumbling upon the "Work and Family" section. There it was in bold print: a suggestion for how working mothers could fit their children into their lives. It said, "When you get home, set a timer for 15 minutes, then curl up with your child to read a book together or just listen to the tales about her day. By the time the buzzer goes off, she'll have had enough of a mom fix that you can start preparing supper."[1]

Welcome to motherhood in the twenty-first century.

Americans now believe that it is the quality, not quantity, of time we spend with our children that matters. We insist that it's fine for mothers to be away from their children all day, every day as long as when they come home at night, they make that one hour with their children really, really count. That's it. That's all there is to raising children. Women actually believe—or have talked themselves into believing—that they can raise children with leftover time, as if the creation of an intelligent, compassionate, confident, hard-working human being doesn't require a vast amount of time and energy, as if a relationship with a child can be built within a certain number of hours we have set aside to make it happen. But it just doesn't work that way. "Being a good parent isn't about measured minutes. It's about relationships, especially the primary love relationship we call 'attachment,'" writes Penelope Leach in *Child* magazine.[2] When mothers do not take the time and put forth the effort required to establish a healthy, working relationship with their children—which can only be accomplished by being with them day in and day out—they will not enjoy the benefits that come from this work.

This is the reason so many working mothers find themselves in endless power struggles with their children. Jane Sullivan, a working mother of two, tells *Newsweek* that her son purposely takes an hour to do homework that shouldn't take more than twenty minutes. "He doesn't see us much, and this is time to act out," says Sullivan, adding, "We have battles in which he tests us. Maybe this is his way of getting us to fully focus on him."[3] Sullivan is not alone. Spend any time at all with the average working mother and you are sure to hear about similar problems. This is the inevitable result when mothers make their children a sideline occupation. Indeed, Americans have made a grave mistake in thinking we can reinvent the way children are raised. Children are not supposed to fit into our lives; we're supposed to fit into theirs. We must begin to accept again the truth about children, no matter how hard it may be to digest: *The number of hours parents spend with their children absolutely, unequivocally, matters.* What children need—what children have always needed—is time and attention, and the undivided loyalty of one adult, preferably their mothers. Anything less just isn't good enough.

The women who know this better than any of us are full-time mothers who were once working mothers. This is an ever-growing group that has been largely overlooked. Jane, a teacher turned full-time mom, compared her current experience of motherhood to that when she was working full-time:

> I know firsthand what a difference time makes with kids. My five-year-old daughter had spent an enormous amount of time on a project for school that she needed my help with and was extremely enthused about it. I know her creation would not have produced the same results had I been "working" because the attention span of a kindergartner would not have allowed her to cram everything into a couple of evenings or a weekend. More importantly, I was there for encouragement and praise along the way. I could say that I would have done this a year ago, but honestly, I would have been trying to accomplish multiple tasks as she was working on it, and depending on the day and my work demands, my entire demeanor would not have been the same. The completion of the task would have carried far more weight than the actual process, going totally against what I tried to teach my own students for so many years. So in the end, it was my time and undivided attention that made the difference.[4]

Another former working mom tells me she remembers "all too well the dreaded morning routine when I was working full-time: a run at 4:45 AM, a 5-minute shower, a 'breakfast' consumed at an unhealthy speed, and then rushing upstairs to push and prod my oldest son along to get dressed and downstairs to eat so I could begin the 7:15 morning commute to work."[5] She adds, "Soon after I quit my job, my son said to me one morning as I was brushing his hair, 'We don't have to hurry, hurry, hurry anymore, Mom.'" The fact is, no mother has the energy or drive to give her children what they need if her energy and drive has been depleted by a day at the office. She is fooling herself to think otherwise. As former working mother Jean Blockhus-Grover says, "Despite my strength with organization, a high degree of energy, and having a husband who is great with doing his part, I often felt as if my head was barely above water." Similarly, Sarah Bridges, a licensed psychologist who quit her job to stay home with her children remembers her life as a working mom: "I didn't like how my kids became items on my to-do list. I hurried through our evenings, dying for the minute they would all go to sleep."[6] Such is the reality of working motherhood.

But it's one thing to read or hear about the lives of working mothers and another thing to come face to face with it. Not long ago I ran into a woman I used to know in my younger years who is now a working mother, and we spent a good part of the evening discussing her life as a mom. Sarah rises each day at 4:30 AM, wakes her three and a half–year-old daughter up sometime before 6:00 AM and begins her forty-minute commute to work. (Breakfast is eaten in the car.) On the way, she and her husband drop their daughter off at day care and pick her up nine or ten hours later to head back home for some "quality time." In order to make room for this, the daughter stays up until 9:00 PM.

As the night wore on, Sarah talked about all the things working mothers do, using all the necessary rationalizations she must in order to keep her sanity: she loves her daughter's day care; she's a better mom for working; she spends a lot of quality time with her daughter (though she would later reveal that, invariably, "all hell breaks loose" after work, making quality time somewhat elusive). And through it all, it was abundantly clear that she was conflicted. She even mentioned that if she and her husband have another child, her husband would have to stay home. (I presume she said it would be her husband be-cause she makes more money, but I certainly didn't ask.) Twice in the evening our conversation was interrupted when her babysitter called to ask her to come home, which was only two houses away. It seems her daughter wouldn't go to sleep without seeing her. (It was, after all, a Friday night; and her daughter hadn't seen her mother all day.) At 11:00 PM, Sarah left for the last time. But she called me at the party to tell me something she hadn't finished telling me earlier because she knew I wanted to share her story in my book. She told me that every week her daughter asks her, "Is it the weekend yet, Mommy?" And on one particular week Sarah asked her daughter what she wanted to do over the weekend, and her daughter replied, "Play in my playroom, stay together, and have a family."

I remember being torn that night. I was struck by Sarah's honesty, since it was obvious that she was not happy with her current arrangement. At one point her eyes began to well up with tears, and it was almost as though she were searching for an answer. And because she was not a stranger to me, I desperately wanted to help her. But I knew that the only answer I could offer would be the one she wouldn't want to hear. So I said nothing.

What I wanted to say was that her daughter needs her. What I wanted to say was that the reason her three-and-a-half–year old was still awake at 11:00 p.m. was that she is hungry for her mother's attention. What I wanted to say was though she considers herself "a better mom for working," her daughter doesn't see it that way. What I wanted to tell her was that that there is plenty of research that concludes that what children want most from their parents is for them to "be there," not just physically but mentally. As Dr. Ron Taffel, a family therapist and author of *The Second Family*, says, "In my conversations with them, children from kindergarten to age twelve overwhelmingly indicate that what they want most is more time, as in undivided attention."[7] He adds, "The quality of family life has changed dramatically."[8] Indeed it has. And the reason for this is that we have dismissed a critical fact: anything worthwhile requires an enormous amount of time, attention, and hard work; and raising children is no exception. If we do not put forth the effort, we cannot reap the rewards. We will only suffer consequences.

Modern-Day Motherhood

It is 2004, and at least 38 percent of American families do not have a parent at home. Gone are the days when babies and toddlers were home with their mothers, when morning meant moving slowly, when children played in their neighborhoods and were called inside at dusk, when TV viewing was limited, when homework was supervised, when bedtime was early, and when illness and obesity was rare. This childhood has been replaced with day care, after-school care, fast food, unlimited TV viewing, latch-key children, countless extra-curricular activities, no downtime, sleep deprivation, and childhood obesity.

The most powerful voices in America would like us to believe that it is a coincidence the well being of our nation's children has declined at the same time there has been a surge of mothers entering the work-force. But this is no coincidence. The needs of children have been severely compromised as a result of mothers choosing to spend the majority of their children's waking hours away from them. The most powerful voices in America also argue that there are many ways to be a good mother, that being at home is only one option. They are correct in pointing out that there are many ways to be a good mother. But women cannot be good at something—or even bad at something—if they are not doing it in the first place. Indeed, the "good mother" is not a perfect mother, as women's groups like to claim. There is no such thing. The "good mother" simply believes that she is primarily responsible for raising the children she brought into the world. Help is fine, even necessary. But choosing to pay someone else to do the bulk of the work for you just because you don't "choose" to do it is not fine. Working mothers cannot expect to get the same results that a full-time mother does without doing the same work. Would any business allow one of its employees to hire someone to do most of her work for her?

Mothering is harder than any other job in the world. Most people have no trouble acknowledging this. But saying this and understanding it are two different things. The truth is that our society does not view raising children as real work. This is particularly evident when we hear people refer to women whose children sleep, eat, or behave well as being "lucky." A mother is "lucky" if her child takes a nap or goes to sleep at night without a fuss; a mother is "lucky" if her child eats fruits and vegetables; a mother is "lucky" if her child behaves well. It is simply easier for us to believe that children become who they are by sheer luck. If we believe this, it means that we can get away with doing less than we should be doing. It means that we can be lazy in our parenting. It also means that when both parents work outside the home and thus neglect their parenting responsibilities, it's okay—because who our children become has less to do with what kind of parents we are than it does with, say, biology.

We are wrong.

Healthy, well-rested, and well-behaved children are the tangible result of a mother's hard work. As hard as it may be for some of us to accept, children are who they are largely because of how their mothers raise them. I am not saying that just because a child doesn't sleep well or is a finicky eater or has behavioral problems that it means a mother isn't doing her job.

On the other hand, maybe it does.

Despite what mass media would have us believe, motherhood has very little to do with pregnancy, childbirth, and maternity leave. It's what comes afterward—the actual childrearing—that matters. This is when the real work begins. Unfortunately, it is also the time when many mothers today quit. And it is simply unreasonable to say that there is no difference between a woman who stays at home to do the work of motherhood and one who doesn't. The only people who would believe this are those who do not appreciate or understand the overwhelming needs of children. So for the purpose of clarification, let's take a look at what these needs are.

Children's Health

One of our most important jobs is to take care of our children's health, which is in our hands from the moment they are born. But we have failed at this task—miserably. While the media is quick to report statistics about sleep deprivation and childhood obesity, what they rarely report is the connection between these problems and the absence of mothers from home. Indeed, journalists frequently furrow their brows and ask experts why such things are happening to today's children. And the response is always the same: children are far too sedentary. They do not get enough exercise and eat too much junk food. Moreover, they spend far too much time in front of the television. What the experts will not mention, however, is why this is so. Because that one small detail—that mothers aren't around to keep their children on track—is simply too much truth to swallow.

Indeed, when today's working mothers ask pediatricians or other experts why their children aren't sleeping, eating, or behaving well, most receive the stereotypical, politically correct response: "Some children need more sleep than others," or "Johnny's metabolism is a little off," or "Johnny is going through an aggressive phase." On the surface, such responses may seem harmless; and they certainly do a lot to assuage a working mother's guilt. But what the experts will not say to these mothers, what they can't say, is that the only way to solve their children's problems is to go home and do the work of motherhood.

They won't say it, but this doesn't make it any less true.

Sleep

Sleep has been one of the first things parents have compromised in their desire to live a fast-paced life. And that's fine—for them. What is not fine is when parents expect children to compromise their sleep. For while we adults may be able to function on a minimal amount of sleep—or at least think we can—children cannot. "A good night's sleep, much like nutrition, seat belts, and a roof over one's head, is an inalienable right of every child and a bona fide parental responsibility," writes Dr. Judith Owens, director of the Pediatric Sleep Disorders Clinic at Brown University School of Medicine.[9] Indeed, any pediatrician or sleep expert can tell you that children need a lot of sleep.

Sleep is as necessary to their physical and emotional health as food and exercise, which is why we must learn to respect and value their need for sleep.

The difference between a child who has had enough sleep and one who hasn't cannot be overstated. A child who is well rested is joyful, content, and happy. A child who is sleep deprived—or just plain tired—is antsy, difficult, and, as Inda Schanen writes in *The 7 O'Clock Bedtime*, "wears his fatigue like a suit of itchy, ill-fitting clothing."[10] Moreover, there is a direct correlation between sleep and behavior. "Kids' behavior is a tell-tale sign of whether or not they're getting enough sleep," writes Dr. Marc Weissbluth, author of *Healthy Sleep Habits, Happy Child*.[11] Unfortunately, many do not see the connection between their children's poor sleep habits and their erratic behavior. "If a child has poor sleep habits, his parents will think that he just doesn't need a lot of sleep. That's probably not true—in fact, it's likely that such a child is actually sleep-deprived," says Dr. Jodi Mindell, sleep expert for Baby Center.com.[12] Although the amount of sleep children need varies somewhat, most experts agree on the following estimates:

> Infants: About 16 hours (2 naps)
> One-year-old: About 14 hours (1 nap)
> Ages 2-4: About 13 hours (1 nap)
> Ages 5-11: About 11 hours
> Ages 12-18: About 9 hours

In the desire to live fast-paced lives, some mothers cut corners on their children's naps—or even stop their naps long before they should. As Diane Fisher observes, "It is unfortunate that our society is impatient with slow, subtle infant schedules in this fast, goal-oriented culture."[13] Nevertheless, full-time moms are at least in a position to give their children naps every day. Working mothers are not. These women are at the mercy of both their bosses and their children's caregivers and are therefore unable to control and monitor their children's sleep habits. This is why their children are notoriously sleep deprived. Children of working mothers are not functioning according to their own body clocks, but according to the needs of their mothers. Indeed, most working mothers wake their children up before their bodies wake naturally and rush them out the door before they're even awake. Furthermore, they are not around during the day to make sure their children take naps. (Children do not get adequate sleep in day care.) Finally, they keep their children up late in the evening because they haven't seen them all day. Add this up, and the result is obvious: sleep deprivation.

There are several ways parents can make sure their children get the sleep they need. (Naturally, this requires that a parent be at home.) Weissbluth and Mindell stress the importance of uninterrupted sleep. This means that if parents want their children to get the sleep they need and if they want them to take a nap and go to sleep at night without a big production, then they need to develop a routine early on—say when their children are around four months old—and stick with it. All babies do not need to be on the same schedule, but they do need to have the same schedule every day. You can't do one thing one day and another thing the next and expect your baby to sleep the way you want him to. Children will only be compliant if they know what to expect. (This same theory can be applied to discipline, which I discuss later.) Children also need good quality naps, say Weissbluth and Mindell. This means they should not be napping in cars and strollers (beyond the newborn stage), and their naps should be at the same time every day in a quiet room with little or no noise in order to get optimal sleep. "Catching" naps here and there will not produce the desired outcome. "Studies in adults have shown that irregular sleep-wake patterns lead to significant alterations in our moods and sense of well-being, and undermine our ability to sleep at the desired times. The same is true of young children, although many parents don't seem to appreciate this fact," writes Richard Ferber in *Solve Your Child's Sleep Problems*.[14]

How can you tell if your child is sleep deprived? If you find yourself waking your child up or if your child falls asleep in the car on a regular basis, and if he wakes up frequently in the middle of the night, then your child is most likely overtired. Moreover, if he seems cranky or irritable during the day or falls asleep much earlier than his usual bedtime, this is also a good sign that he is sleep deprived. Weissbluth also points out that most kids who don't sleep well are going to bed too late. He notes that many parents make the mistake of thinking that if they keep their children up or if their children skip their naps every now and then that they will become so tired that they'll just fall into bed at night, the way an adult might, but it doesn't work that way. "The better rested kids are, the easier it is for them to fall asleep, and the easier it is for them to stay asleep longer."[15] Once again, this is where working mothers are at a loss, as many parents keep their children up at night because they haven't seen them all day. But children have their own system, and it is up to us to work around it.

Food

Perhaps the most significant fallout of working motherhood is our children's poor eating habits. Once again, it is fine if adults want to subsist on a grab-and-go diet, but it is not fine to ask children to do the same. Depriving children of the proper nutrition—the kind that you and I had as children—is pure and simple neglect. Nutrition is as critical to a child's emotional and physical development as sleep. "Like sleep, food is not optional in life, but its quality is," writes Inda Schaenan.[16] Unfortunately, many parents do not think nutrition is important; and even if they do, they aren't around to do anything about it anyway. As Reich notes, "Working parents arrive home long after the stomachs of children demand to be filled."[17] For these families, dinnertime can be as elusive as breakfast, and many parents resort to convenience foods. Lucky for them, they have plenty of support for doing so. Virtually every food commercial or advertisement makes sure to add that such-and-such food can be prepared in fifteen minutes or less. Moreover, supermarkets now offer meals in which all the work has already been done. All parents need to do is know how to operate a microwave. Thus, the life of a working mother is now even easier. Easier, that is, until her guilty conscience gets the better of her, and she realizes she should probably spend some time in the kitchen if she expects her children to be healthy. But, of course, she can't. She doesn't have time. "Cutting, chopping dragging out the pans, sautéing, boiling, and broiling are not pleasures during the week. Besides, you have to change your clothes so you don't get the suit messed up—but if you're late getting home, then you don't have time to change, and if you're eating fast to run to parents' night at school, then you barely have time to eat anyway," writes Goldman.[18] Goldman's suggestion for working mothers? "Don't get bent out of shape when your kid won't eat the dinner. You don't have that much emotion invested in it in the first place. Point to the options: the boxes of cereal."[19] And it is exactly this kind of thinking that has caused our children's health to decline. Indeed, researchers at Pennsylvania State University studied the eating habits of seven-year-old girls and their mothers and found that the fussy eaters tended to be children whose "mothers didn't have much time to help their kids eat healthy, so instead of trying to feed them a wide variety of foods, the moms would offer foods they knew their children would eat."[20] Naturally, such foods are often high in salt, sugar, and fat.

The reality is that teaching children how to eat is an enormous task. If you want to do it right, you have to spend several hours a day in the kitchen. There is no shortcut. It is because many mothers don't have the time or patience for this that they allow their children to do as they please when it comes to food. After all, it's tedious to sit down with a toddler or young child three times a day and make sure the fruits and vegetables get from the plate to the mouth when all children really want is dessert. As Leann Birch, a psychologist at Penn State University, writes, "Most children reject things at first. It takes multiple exposures—sometimes as many as ten times—before kids come to accept and like new foods they initially turned down."[21] Indeed, this is one of the things that makes parenting so difficult and is the reason some women choose not to deal with it. And the results of their lackadaisical attitude are evident. "According to the latest federal figures, the percentage of youngsters ages 6-11 who are overweight has tripled since the 1960s," writes Shannon Brownlee on Time.com. [22]

The percentage of overweight children has *tripled* since the 1960s. (Wasn't that when mothers began to leave their homes in search of greener pastures?) Brownlee adds that the Surgeon General "issued an urgent call for the nation to fight its growing weight problem" and discusses the even more alarming number of children with diabetes.[23] Brownlee's suggestion for parents is to not let their kids get into the habit of eating high-fat, high-sugar foods and out of the habit of getting regular exercise. Well, yes, this is obvious. But the only way this can occur is if a parent is home to see that it happens. Naturally, the article neglects to mention that part.

There are several ways to make sure children eat well, maintain a balanced diet, and avoid overeating. None of the following suggestions is original, by the way, but it's the kind of information that is hard to come by today because we rarely hear from full-time moms, who have the most experience in dealing with children. To begin with, women have to accept that they must spend several hours a day in the kitchen, not because their meals need to be elaborate but because planning meals, cooking the food, and sitting down with our children to make sure they eat what we've prepared is enormously time-consuming. I personally spend about three-and-a-half hours a day in the kitchen, not because I am a great cook, but because I sit down and eat meals with my daughter. And nine out of ten times, I finish first and spend the subsequent thirty minutes talking, playing, or cajoling her to eat her food. This is exactly what I mean when I refer to motherhood as work. Who else is going to go to such lengths except us moms?

Second, it is important that we start babies off on the right track. As soon as they begin eating solid foods, we should introduce healthy foods rather than sugary foods. "It is very easy to introduce new foods to kids between about 9 and 18 months, when they are putting anything in their mouth,"[24] says Dr. Susan B. Roberts, professor of nutrition and psychiatry at Tufts University. The good news is that if a baby has never had anything sugary, he will not have anything to compare the "good" foods with, so even if the baby doesn't take to the healthy foods right away, he probably will eventually. After all, anything different from formula will taste marvelous. "Kids are born with a sweet tooth, but they have to learn to enjoy other tastes," says Birch.[25]

Third, try not to have the foods children crave in the house and make sure to eat balanced meals yourself. Believe it or not, babies and toddlers usually do exactly as their parents do, so if we prepare three healthy meals a day, as opposed to "grazing" throughout the day, children will follow our lead. It will be the only pattern they know. "Everyone grows up with food preferences that are largely programmed by the foods around them," says Roberts. "So what you put on your table, and what children see their parents eating and enjoying, has a big influence."[26] I introduced my daughter to Shredded Wheat very early on (allowing the squares to get soggy in the milk) when I couldn't get her to eat oatmeal. She took to it because it was something different and I think this alone made it appealing. Several months down the road, however, I bought Honeycomb cereal for myself. My plan was not to give any to my daughter not because I think it is harmful, but because I knew that as long as Honeycomb was an option, she would choose it over the Shredded Wheat. But I relented in a weak moment (as all moms do) and gave her a few pieces to snack on. Big mistake. As long as she saw that box of Honeycomb on top of the refrigerator, that was all she wanted. So much for the Shredded Wheat. But I did not want to undo all of my hard work, so I never bought Honeycomb again (much to my dismay), and my daughter quickly went back to the Shredded Wheat. Out of sight, out of mind.

Fourth, feed your children when they're hungry—which means not letting them snack throughout the day. This is hard to do, because food tends to keep babies and toddlers happy and content. But there are foods we can give them—raisins, grapes, Cheerios—that will probably not fill them up to the point where they won't eat at mealtime. (Unless, of course, these snacks were the meal.) Because if children eat loads of bread and Animal Crackers and muffins in between meals, they absolutely will not eat at mealtime. This is just basic common sense.

Lastly, make mealtime a big deal, the way it used to be when we were growing up. (As I said, it doesn't have to be as elaborate as our own mothers' meals, but it should take some effort.) Unfortunately, cooking is today as foreign to full-time moms as it is to working moms. But the difference is that full-time moms can invest in learning this skill because they are not rushed all the time. Since they are focused on doing one job well, they can teach their children good eating habits, which will last them a lifetime. This is a gift of huge proportions, particularly in this age of overindulgence.

None of this is to suggest that there is anything wrong with having sweets or pizza or hot dogs or whatever. After all, what's childhood without these yummy things? I love sweets. I cannot go a day without them, and I allow my daughter to eat them. But she doesn't get them unless she's eaten the healthy foods first. And if she doesn't eat the fruits and vegetables, then she doesn't get the sweets. Again, there is nothing particularly new about this. Most of us probably remember our mothers telling us that we couldn't leave the table until we finished our milk and that if we didn't finish our dinner, there would be no dessert. So it's not as though I've discovered something, and I am not suggesting that just because a mother does these things that her children will always be compliant. But, believe me, it is well worth the effort, because you won't have to worry as much about the constant array of snacks and treats your children will get when they're in other people's care. At least you'll know they've had the good stuff.

Exercise

Americans get an earful about the science of exercise but, quite frankly, all I know or care about is that when I work out, I feel great, and when I don't, I feel awful. I also know, as most parents do, that the same holds true for children. When my daughter has had a good brisk walk or has played hard, she sleeps better. And when she sleeps better, she behaves better. And that makes Mama very happy. I also know that when she is running around, preferably outside, she is at her happiest. Nothing gets her going like a lot of running around.

My daughter is not unique. I have been around children my entire life, and I can honestly say that no matter what the age, there is something medicinal about being outside in the fresh air. Exercise is a natural stimulant that keeps the brain functioning well and keeps our moods in check. In the old days, children got plenty of exercise. I remember my mother always telling me to "go outside and play" or "find something to do outside" if I was ever bored on a Saturday. In those days, kids would play outside with their neighbors after school. Today's neighborhoods, on the other hand, are desolate. Games of tag are no more. Instead children are inside, sitting in front of a television set or computer screen, usually eating. And this problem has such far-reaching consequences (I discuss this in greater detail in the next section) that it alone is a reason for mothers to come home.

Discipline

Discipline is a vital part of the work of motherhood. Unfortunately, it causes many parents great distress. The tough love approach parents used to take has been replaced with the feel-good approach the baby boomers began. During the 1960s and 1970s, discipline became a bad word. Discipline stifles children's creativity, said the boomers. Children need choices; they need to feel free to be themselves. The reason for the backlash was that many children had grown up at a time when the answer to their questions was, "Because I said so." And I admit it: I hate that response. So did the Boomers. Unfortunately, their alternative was no better. They decided to be their children's friends rather than their parents. They believed that "talking it out" was a better method. "Something happened to parenting as the job shifted from the World War II generation to its children, the baby boomers. They put less emphasis on rules and more on self-esteem. Where previous generations were restrictive, baby boomers were permissive. Where previous generations gave orders, baby boomers negotiated. Mothers and fathers had been parents. Baby boomers became co-equals, playmates. And we're seeing the fruit of that approach. We're seeing kids who are disconnected, disaffected, materialistic, filled with a misplaced sense of entitlement and sometimes, just flat-out spoiled," writes Washington writer Leonard Pitts Jr.[27] Indeed, the result of this approach has been all too evident in our nation's schools and in many homes across the country. Simply put, the philosophy failed. Until we are able to find a middle ground between "Cause I said so!" and "How does that make you feel?" parents and children will continue to suffer.

The truth is, discipline is not as complicated as we have made it. It is challenging, to be sure, and it requires an enormous amount of patience and consistency, but it's not complicated. The work involved in disciplining one's children is, to a large extent, the same work a teacher does with his or her students. And as a parent and an educator, it has become abundantly clear to me that all children need four basic things from adults in order to be well disciplined. We must be calm when giving orders, know when to ignore certain behavior, reward good behavior, and be consistent in everything we do and say. Doing these things allows children to feel safe, and this safety ultimately allows them to be in control of themselves and their lives. But in order for them to be able to do this, parents have to be in control first. Too many people think of discipline as being only about punishment. But it is not. "Discipline is only in small part about punishment; in large part, it is about building character, testing self-esteem, and teaching social skills that will ultimately create a *self-disciplined* adolescent and adult," writes best-selling author Michael Gurian.[28]

Once parents accept this and are not afraid of it, they will be able to let go of the idea that discipline is a bad thing. "When discipline is seen as teaching and is conveyed with a great deal of empathy and nurturing care, children feel good when they comply. It is a warm, nourishing feeling to feel that you are the gleam in someone else's eye," writes Stanley Greenspan in *The Irreducible Needs of Children*.[29] When we discipline children responsibly, we prove to them how much we love them and care about their well being. When we continually negotiate or allow them to have their way, we tell them, in effect, that they are in charge of us. And, believe it or not, children don't want to be in charge of us, no matter how many times they tell us they do and no matter how old they are. I've seen this again and again in my teaching experience. Most kids who exhibit behavior problems are crying out for order. What seems like strictness to us is comfort for them. As Gurian puts it, "A child learns to be an authority by modeling after others who hold clear and competent authority. It is the child raised by people without strength who becomes weak. It is the child raised with high expectations who becomes independent."[30]

Discipline begets discipline. Adults who have good self-discipline will have less trouble disciplining their children because it comes naturally to them. Just as unorganized, unscheduled, or overweight parents tend to produce unorganized, unscheduled, or overweight children, parents who do not eat, sleep, or behave well themselves struggle with their children when it comes to food, sleep, and good behavior. Indeed, psychologists and pediatricians have pointed out that parents have told them that they want their children to eat well despite the fact that they do not eat well themselves. Similarly, if parents themselves are lax, they will most assuredly have trouble disciplining their children.

That said, there will always be some parents who are better than others at disciplining their children, just as some teachers are better at this than others. What has changed is that so many mothers are not at home with their children, and this has two specific consequences. First, working mothers are far more likely to experience power struggles with their children because they have not been around from the beginning, on a consistent basis, to instill their own discipline. Instead, they are forced to rely on others to do this work for them. The children of these mothers, confused about the boundaries of good behavior, often lash out. Indeed, the reality of the mother-child relationship is that a mother has to earn the right to be obeyed, and this will only occur if she is present in her children's lives. If she makes this investment, she will reap the rewards of her hard work. But if she has passed this work off to someone else, she will not.

Second, working mothers are much less inclined to discipline their children during the hours they are with them for the simple reason that they haven't seen them all day and do not want to spend what little time they do have fighting with their kids. "Working parents have a very tough time thinking about limits. Their ability to set limits has gone way down in this generation. Parents tell me, 'I can't stand to be away all day and then come back and be the disciplinarian,'" writes T. Berry Brazleton.[31] Greenspan notes that "parents don't feel that they have earned the right to set limits. If you feel that you are not there enough for your children, you might not feel right asking that child to be quiet while you talk to Dad about something important."[32] The reason for this is that working mothers are exhausted. Because their nights and weekends are consumed with chores and activities and because they are exhausted from their workday, they simply cannot muster the energy that it takes to discipline their children in a healthy, consistent fashion. Indeed, discipline requires an enormous amount of patience, as mothers are forced to repeat themselves until they're blue in the face. And if mothers are constantly distracted by the demands of the workplace and all the other work they have to get done, there's no way they'll be able to discipline their children well. "It's easier to keep your temper when you don't have a train to catch," writes Gurdon.[33] This is why working mothers are notorious for giving in to whatever their children want just so they can have some peace and quiet. Their bodies crave it.

School and Homework

After I quit teaching, I worked from home as an educational consultant. This involved tutoring kids who were struggling in school and working with their families to understand the reasons for their children's lack of motivation. I can think of only two students—two—who had mothers at home. Most were on their own after school. They were either picked up by babysitters or friends' mothers and were dropped off at home—alone—or they went to a friend's house. The rest of the day would be spent in front of some technological device: a television, computer games, or the Internet. The two students whose mothers were at home were clearly at an advantage. Homework, not television, became their primary focus. And there is simply no question that the constancy these mothers provided was the one and only thing that kept these children on their toes.

In all the years I worked with children, I rarely came across a low-achieving student or a student who exhibited an unusual behavior problem who had a parent at home. Indeed, any good educator can tell you that parental involvement—in which working mothers are notoriously lacking—is critical to a child's success in school. It is rare that one finds a good student who doesn't have a strong parent in his court. As Susan Sherrod writes, "Studies have indicated that children whose parents and/or significant adults share in their formal education tend to do better in school," adding, "Children need and want their families to be involved in their lives."[34] This is true even of the most challenging teenagers who insist that they would love their parents to stay out of their lives. In fact, this may be the most important time for children to have parents at home. The teenage years are a time of great struggle, for both children and parents, and it is critical that teenagers have consistency and order in their lives. After all, we have seen on the nightly news what can happen when they don't get it.

That said, I did come across full-time mothers who were not particularly helpful as far as their children's education was concerned. But it was rare. More often than not, I found myself having to track down the mom or dad and often felt as though I were hounding them about their children. And while I also came across well-meaning working mothers who wanted very much to help their children get on the right track, the problem was that they were not able to make the connection between their children's school problems and their lack of availability to their children after 3:00 PM. So there was rarely any progress. Being involved in your children's school life is part of parenting, and it is just one more thing that takes a back seat in dual-income households. Indeed, homework can become the bane of a working mother's existence. As Melissa Kantor writes in *Working Mother*, "More assignments plus less time equal lots of arguments with your school-age kids. What's a working mom to do?" She goes on to say that the level of homework has increased over the years and that working mothers can't keep up with it: "[Homework] puts working mothers at a disadvantage. More homework plus harder assignments plus a mom who's not getting home until dinnertime equals guilt, stress, and fights."[35]

The common thread in making sure our children's needs are met is consistency. Consistency *is the controlling factor* in the health and well-being of our children. "Consistency is the most important element in your relationship with your children, yet it is the most frequently omitted," writes Sal Severe in *How To Behave So Your Children Will Too*.[36] More than anything else, children want and need to know that they can count on us to do the same things tomorrow that we did today, and that we will ask the same things of them tomorrow that we did today. This is comforting to them, regardless of their age. As an example, my daughter and I have a routine at bedtime where I hold her "one more minute" and then put her down. Then I tell her I love her. And one night she said, "And Daddy loves you." (The "you" means her). And I would say, "Yes, and Daddy loves you." And so began our routine. Then one night when I kissed her and told her I loved her, I forgot to mention Daddy and proceeded to walk out of the room. She then began to cry and in between sobs she was saying something, but I couldn't make it out. Then I finally heard her. She was screaming, "Daddy loves you, Daddy loves you!" So I had to go back into her room to assure that yes, "Daddy loves you, too." She immediately stopped crying and went to sleep.

Older children are just as hungry for consistency. They want their mothers at home with them, first and foremost. They want to connect with them emotionally, and they need us to be in charge of them—overseeing their health, behavior, and education. When we fail to do this, our children suffer. Each time we change our children's surroundings, or change the rules, they react negatively. Though they may not show their reaction immediately, one day they exhibit behavior that we don't understand. Some children may wet their beds; others may show signs of developmental delays or become defiant; some have trouble getting along with other children. Regardless of the symptoms, the underlying problem is usually the same: a lack of consistency.

Unfortunately, this need for consistency is grossly undervalued in our society. We just don't appreciate that the best chance children have for happiness and success is through the relationship they have built with their parents. This relationship takes years to develop, and it cannot be strengthened if parents and children are separated from each other most of the time. Naturally, anyone can be lax or lazy in their parenting—whether they are home full-time or not. But it is indisputable that working parents are at a great disadvantage because they just aren't around. When a mother is not physically available, there is no way she can maintain consistency in her childrearing. Inevitably she will be forced to contend with discrepancies between what she would do in a given situation and what her children's caregivers would do in the same situation. If a mother is trying to get her children to eat better, for example, she will have to depend on other women to carry this out. And when a day care provider has many other children to tend and the child is begging her for cookies, she is not going to care about a mother's desire for her child to have better eating habits. A day care provider's primary concern is damage control. If cookies are what it takes, then cookies it will be.

Life After School

Americans have greatly underestimated the importance of the hours children are not in school, that elusive yet critical time between 3:00 PM and bedtime during which a parent should be, well, parenting. Indeed, we can attribute the surge of problems young people have today to what now takes place during this time of day.

Part of the reason for this is that there is now a common perception that children only need their parents during the early years. Once children begin school, we say, a mother's job is done. She can resume her career. But how many careers or jobs do you know that allow a person to leave at 3:00 PM? And even if you can, the chances are great that you'll have to bring your work home with you. (Even teachers are not exempt from this—unless they've been teaching the same course at the same school year after year.)

Some mothers have even argued that their job doesn't begin until their children are in school. For while a child's early years are all about eating and sleeping and diapers and toilet training and schedules and activities, their later years are about eating and sleeping and schedules and activities and homework and school and transportation and clothes and friends. The needs of children change, but they do not diminish. As one former working mother says, "Babies' needs are pretty simple. But older kids require more: You've got to watch who they're bringing home; their homework gets more complex; and they have activities. It becomes more difficult to delegate that supervision to someone else." [37]

School age children need a parent physically available every hour they are not in school. They should not be waking up to two parents whose attentions are focused on getting ready for work; they should be waking up to one parent who is focused solely on getting them ready for school. For the parents, this means allowing children to wake up slowly, taking the time to help them get dressed, feeding them a healthy breakfast, enjoying spontaneous conversation, making sure they have the materials they need for school, and then driving them (or sending them off) to school. It also means having a parent available during the school day to stop whatever it is he or she is doing in case the child becomes sick or needs something. But most important, it means having a parent available from 3:00 PM. until bedtime, because this is when the true parenting takes place. This is the time when children should be involved with extra-curricular activities, or doing homework, or running around outside, or talking with their mothers about something that happened at school, or going shopping with mom, or helping mom prepare dinner.

This is not what children are doing today. Today's children fend for themselves after school. And with the exception of motivated teenagers, who often stay after school to do various projects and activities, most children end up in extended-day programs (which basically means hanging out until their parents pick them up three hours later), or they go home to an empty house. And it is those who go home to an empty house—latch-key kids, we call them—who are the most vulnerable to becoming overweight or depressed or doing poorly in school.

Out of concern for one of these problems, obesity, Oprah interviewed Melinda Southern, a pediatric physiologist and director for the Pediatric Obesity Clinical Research Section of the Louisiana State

University Medical Center. Southern claimed that children are becoming heavier because of a decrease in physical activity made possible by modern transportation, television, computers, and video games, combined with the availability of high-caloric foods such as fast food, convenience foods and snacks. "Most children who become overweight and obese have a perfectly normal metabolism. The problem isn't their genes, but their environment," says Southern. [38]

Southern spoke with two of Oprah's guests, a mother and her overweight son. She asked them a series of questions about a typical day at their house and what the son did after school. The scenario went like this: Her son was alone after school or sometimes with his older sister or aunt. He watched television. The mother arrived home around dinnertime. When Southern tried to explain all the ways in which the mother could fix the problem with her son's weight—make sure he gets outside every day or is involved in some type of sporting activity—the mother explained that she could not be there to watch over him every minute because she works. Furthermore, she said, her son doesn't have any interest in being outside; he likes to do nothing. No matter what Southern suggested, the mother couldn't hear it. And the reason she couldn't is that the only way for her to help her son would be for her to quit her job and come home.

Television

Here's something to shock us into reality: According to a major study done by the Kaiser Family Foundation, the typical American child spends about five and a half hours a day "consuming" media (computers and music, but mainly TV); and for kids ages eight and older, the time jumps to almost seven hours a day. [39]

Seven hours a day. That's almost a full workday.

Adults who spend a great deal of time in front of the television set know that it is, by and large, a colossal waste of time. And because of its allure, some parents have chosen not to own a television set at all. (We don't go quite this far in our house.) This may seem like a drastic measure, but drastic situations sometimes call for drastic measures. And by my calculations, children watching up to seven hours of television a day is a drastic situation. This does not mean that all parents have to get rid of their television sets. But because it is a constant temptation, begging us every day to avoid more productive activities, parents have a responsibility to teach their children how to use television wisely. Because even if children spend four hours a day in front of the History Channel, they are still wasting time. As Inda Schaenen writes, "Even if television were a great thing, watching it still takes time away from the activities that really matter, and renders [children] less and less capable of entertaining themselves."[40] Furthermore, when children spend so much time consuming media, they spend that much less time with their parents. According to Families Interested in Responsible Media, a non-profit organization dedicated to helping families deal with today's media, parents spend approximately seventeen hours a week with their children, while their children spend up to forty hours a week consuming media. One would think working parents would be that much more inclined to turn off their television sets, given what little time they spend with their children. But the truth is that when exhaustion hits and there's still more work to be done around the house, television is a godsend to the working parent. "In a recent poll by Common Sense Media, 66% of parents felt they could do a better job of monitoring their children's TV habits. Yet at the same time, almost half of all kids have no rules governing how long they're in front of the tube. These seeming contradictions are no doubt due to the incredible power of TV to entertain our children and keep them quiet."[41]

Here again previous generations were at a distinct advantage. Families either didn't have television, or they owned one set and had five channels from which to choose. As a result, television was a family activity. The entire family had to share the one set, and it was easier for parents to control what their children watched. Furthermore, they didn't have to worry about their children "channel surfing." Today, not only do cable and digital television provide families with over fifty channels, many families have a television set in almost every room in the house, including the children's bedrooms. This takes the power out of the hands of the adults and puts it directly into the hands of children. It also keeps families from spending time together.

For parents of toddlers, the allure of television is even greater since children this age demand a great deal of attention. Surely we have all used television as a babysitter at one time or another and wondered what on earth mothers did before there was television. But there is a difference between plopping our children in front of the tube for a half an hour while we do whatever we need to do and leaving them there for hours on end, or allowing them to watch an hour here and an hour there, only to realize that we've allowed them to watch three to four hours of television in one day. Mothers who give in to this temptation know that it's not a good idea. They are well aware that they are choosing to be lazy; they even have pangs of guilt to remind them. But I think there's more to it than laziness. I think some people honestly believe that this is what most kids want to do. But it isn't.

Hard as it is to believe, children are not automatically programmed to want television. The only reason it seems that way to us is because we have grown up with television and in many homes, the television is always on—even when we're not watching it. But it only takes turning off the TV to see how wrong we are about children. Sure, they'll bark at first—after all, we've gotten them used to television—but if you stick to it, you'd be amazed at all the wonderful things that can happen. Lisa Sharkey, a producer for *Good Morning America*, proved just what can happen when we turn off the television (and computers and videos). Sharkey turned off the television for one month, a decision that was immediately protested by her eight and ten-year old sons. But by the end of the first day "an amazing transformation began to take place," she wrote in *Child* magazine.[42] Her younger son began reading a book and in that book the characters were playing Parcheesi, so he decided to get out the family's Parcheesi set, which had been gathering dust.

Sharkey and her sons set the game up on the floor of the bathroom while Sharkey bathed her two-year-old daughter and forty-five minutes later, they were all still in the bathroom playing together. Sometime later, her older son's teacher told her that his reading was improving "by leaps and bounds" and asked Sharkey whether or not she had been doing anything differently at home.[43]

What's important to recognize is that while television can appear to be a mother's best friend during those difficult mothering moments, giving in to it ultimately makes our job harder. When we put a whiny child in front of the television set or computer screen, this will indeed subdue him and thus give us a moment of peace. But what ends up happening in the long run is that children become even more whiny and defiant. This is the effect television has on children. The more they watch, the more they will expect to be able to watch. Children are amazingly adept at reading their parents. They know that if they whine or scream loudly enough, you will put them in front of the television set. Until they learn that their whining will not produce this result, they will continue to whine. They will only stop when they learn that their efforts are futile. Naturally, this means that you have to remain firm. My suggestion is that the next time you are in a TV predicament, muster all the energy you can to ignore your child's incessant whining and, whatever you do, do not turn on the television set. Just pretend you live in the old days and see what happens.

It is important to be able to "read" your children when it comes to television. Often you'll find that a half hour of *Spot* or *Mister Rogers* can be fun and even harmless, but if you leave your child there for too long, you'll notice that a kind of haze envelops them. And then when you ask them a question, they don't hear you. This is when it's time to turn the television off. (Actually, you should turn it off long before this haze develops.) Interestingly enough, you will probably notice that your child isn't even interested in the program after half an hour. He's probably only sitting there because you're letting him. After all, children are notorious for their short attention spans. It is usually difficult for them to engage themselves in the same activity for a long period of time, but the difference with television is that it works as a stimulant—which is why too much of it will definitely have long-lasting effects on their behavior and their ability to concentrate.

The bottom line is that television is just not a good thing. And while it isn't necessary to remove television from your life entirely, it is critical that we are conscious of how much time we spend in front of a device that does little else but cause one to become catatonic. Indeed, "the joy of reading or conversing is far more satisfying than the old electronic TV drip ever was, and the sounds of your own real-life existence are far more engaging than the chatter of make-believe people," writes Yonason Goldson.[44]

Overscheduling

Overscheduling is the term we came up with to describe the number of activities today's children are involved in. Many children now participate in so many activities that they have no time to relax and play. Somewhere along the line, parents decided that packing in as many organized activities will somehow make for smarter or more accomplished children—but it doesn't. All it does is put an emphasis on outward achievement and competition, which are only healthy when they are part of a child's life, not when they consume a child's life. (Consider what we know about the private lives of geniuses. Such pressure is entirely unhealthy for children.) Indeed, what today's parents dismiss is the absolute necessity of good old-fashioned boredom. If children had the opportunity to be productive on their own, without having every moment filled in with unnecessary planned activities, parents would be amazed at how bright and creative their children could become. As Inda Schaenan puts it: "Yes, I do want my child to be bored. I want all my children to confront boredom, to come up against that blank wall of time and to have to find a way through that appeals to them as individuals. I do not want their lives so full and so fully planned that they never have to think about what to do next."[45]

But it isn't just the desire to have well-rounded children that leads parents to overschedule their kids. Working parents use these activities as a way of keeping their children occupied while they are at work. "Try as we might to suggest that all these enrichment activities are for the good of children, there is ample evidence that they are really for the convenience of parents with way too little leisure time of their own," writes Anna Quindlen.[46]

Helping our children organize their after-school lives and just being around is part of our job as parents. This is the time when children need someone to help them with their schoolwork, drive them to an extra-curricular activity and help cheer them on, talk through their problems, and answer questions. But, as Shaenan writes, "Some parents fill up their children's lives with classes and activities in order to avoid direct contact with their children, the kind of contact that is often grueling, frustrating, menial, laborious, and exhausting."[48]

Suffice it to say, the work of motherhood is no small task. For those who want to know what it is that full-time mothers do all day, this is it. Children who eat, sleep, and behave well and who are successful in school are not accidents. Nor do they turn out this way because they simply have better mothers. They turn out this way because they have mothers who are willing to do the work of motherhood. Any woman who puts forth this same effort will reap these same rewards. As Woody Allen once said, "Eighty percent of success is showing up."[49]

≈)

"My Children Just Love Day Care."

> You can't pay someone to do for a child what a
> parent will do for free. Even excellent child care
> can never do what a good parent can do.
>
> Urie Bronfenbrenner

C HILDREN BELIEVE WHAT THEY ARE TAUGHT TO BELIEVE and
become what they are taught to become. Indeed, the power
adults have is almost frightening. Unfortunately, it is impossible to appreciate or understand this unless you are with children
every day. The reason working mothers are able to do what they do is
that they live in a state of ignorant bliss. They do not realize that by
being away from their children all day, every day, they are choosing to
allow their power to be substituted—and often even undermined—by
those with whom they leave their children. Because whom a child
spends the majority of his waking hours with will have an enormous
impact on his personality, his character, and his soul. It's inevitable.

You would think this fact alone would keep women from using
nannies and day care centers on a full-time basis, barring the most
extreme circumstances. But it doesn't. It would, perhaps, if women

were aware of how vital their presence is in their children's lives. But this is not the message women hear about motherhood. Instead they are told that it is perfectly all right to return to work if that is their choice, that every woman has an inherent right to pay other people to raise her children. Women now feel entitled to give up their parenting responsibilities. Moreover, they do not view raising children as an actual career, so they disregard the work to be done once they bring children into the world, or they assume such work can be performed by almost anyone.

And it cannot. No matter how much working mothers wish it weren't true, the reality is that there is no substitute for a parent at home. Indeed, the casual manner in which we now pass our children off to strangers is downright embarrassing—and insulting to children. We have chosen to place our faith in day care in the face of the overwhelming evidence of its harmful effects and the experience of most women, who suffer immediate pangs of guilt and anxiety dropping off their six-week–old newborns at day care centers. "When we choose to put a child in day care, we want to believe it's good, and so we do," writes Covey. He adds, "That which we desire most earnestly, we believe most easily."[1]

That which we desire most earnestly, we believe most easily.

Welcome to the world of working mothers. Their guilt and stress is of their own making, and they get through their day with rationalizations. To give you an idea of how deep the rationalizations run, consider two of the working mothers Susan Chira describes in *A Mother's Place.* One woman tells her, "My goal is to get home by 7:30 PM. My feeling is, if you miss bedtime, you blow it."[2] In this woman's distorted view of motherhood, she thinks it's okay to be absent from her children's lives as long as she wants to—*assuming* she shows up for bedtime. If she doesn't show up then, she's blown it. Chira then introduces a friend of hers who she says has "responsibilities that often keep her at the office until 8:00 or 9:00 PM"[3] But no matter, says Chira, because "her half hour at her daughters' bedtime gives her a sense of intimacy and assurance that is evident every time I have seen her with her children."[4]

Working mothers can grasp at all the straws they want. Not only does the research on day care—or on children who are separated from their mothers for long periods of time—show its overwhelmingly negative effects, but no reasonable person can believe that there's no difference between the type of "mothering" Chira and her friends think they do and the kind of mothering that takes place throughout the day, all week long. As Judith Wallerstein writes in *The Unexpected Legacy of Divorce*, "Being fed and put to bed is a tiny fraction of what [children] need. Parents must provide time and energy to talk, play, read, and pay attention to their young children." What working mothers do not seem to recognize is that a child bonds with his mother as part of their daily routine. This relationship is delicate and time-intensive. It is "not a quick bonding period—one that fits into today's typical twelve-week maternity leave. Rather, it is a slow, gradual process of many seemingly trivial communication cues and responses," says Diane Fisher in testimony regarding infant brain development.[5] When children have one adult they can depend on, when they hear the same voice talking to them and teaching them every day, they grow to feel worthy of love, secure in who they are and in what they are capable of becoming.

The unfortunate reality is that society has chosen to make motherhood an issue of what mothers need rather than what children need. Consequently, today's children are growing up without a childhood, an honest to goodness childhood—complete with mothers who would rather be with them than anywhere else in the world. And we would rather bury our heads in the sand and pretend this doesn't matter than create a better life for our children. Indeed, society doesn't require women to actually *do* the work of motherhood in order to be deemed good mothers. All they have to do to is make it through childbirth and provide their children with food, clothing, and a place to sleep. The rest is superfluous.

Perhaps the greatest argument—defense, really—put forth by women about why it's acceptable for mothers to work outside the home is that some mothers are simply unhappy at home; therefore, their children are better off being raised by others. This has a certain logic, but the truth is more complicated. The argument overlooks that most women today make up their minds, before they've even given birth, about whether they'll return to the workforce. So how could they possibly know whether they would be happy at home? Indeed, there are far more women who thought they would go back to work but later changed their minds than there are women who thought they would stay home only to change their minds and go back to work. Very few mothers stay home with their children only to realize two or three years into it that they are miserable and want to return to the workforce. Therefore, it is unreasonable to argue that some women just "know" they couldn't handle being at home. They've never given motherhood a chance.

Psychologists and child care experts have acknowledged that even marginal care at home is better than day care. "A home must be very bad before it can be bettered by a good institution," writes reknowned psychiatrist John Bowlby.[6] Despite what working mothers claim, an unfulfilled full-time mother does not automatically make her a bad mother; it just makes her an unfulfilled woman. There's a difference. Unless she's causing her children physical or mental harm, her children don't really care whether she's happy and fulfilled. They only care about whether she loves them enough to be with them most of the time. This theory goes back many years. In the movie *Gone With the Wind*—released in the 1930s—Rhett Butler takes his daughter on an extended trip to get her away from Scarlett, a spoiled, petulant woman who was never happy with what she had and who was a terrible mother. Rhett was clearly the better parent, and he thought he was doing right by keeping his daughter from her "bad mother." Several weeks into the trip, however, his daughter wanted to go home. It seems that despite her mother's selfish ways, she missed her mother terribly.

When Rhett returns, he says to Scarlett, "Apparently, any mother—even a bad mother—is better than no mother at all."[7]

Of course, this is not a popular theory today, as many women are convinced that children of semi-happy full-time mothers are better off away from their mothers. In fact, it is this philosophy that has resulted in the ever-famous claim, "I'm a better mom for working." Of course, it is true that if a woman is depressed, her attitude and behavior will negatively affect those around her. Anyone who has known someone with depression understands this. But to suggest that depressed at-home mothers are in any way the norm, or that full-time motherhood makes women more susceptible to depression (the postpartum period notwithstanding) is absurd. As Susan Chira writes, "Researchers found that the more dissatisfied a woman was with her home life, the more depressed she tended to be. Working women, on the other hand, felt less depressed about troubles at home than did housewives."[8] What Chira conveniently overlooks about this "research" is that there are many reasons why a woman at home may be dissatisfied. Chira presumes that a full-time mom's depression has to do with her motherhood role when in fact it is much more likely that it has to do with her marriage. (Remember Betty Friedan?) And while most people can appreciate the relief that work can bring in such circumstances, if you're a mother of young children, "going to work" to escape your problems is not going to solve anything. In fact, it will only add to them, for you will then have to deal with the fallout of working motherhood. Indeed, "going to work" may seem to be the solution for the unhappy at-home mother— as Chira suggests—but it is not. What she will find, in most cases, is that she's robbed Peter to pay Paul. She may have solved her immediate woes, but she will later confront a whole new set of problems, as she finds herself moving Johnny from place to place because she's unhappy with the day care she's chosen. Or when her nanny quits—again. Or when she finds that Johnny is showing signs of behavior problems. Or when she finds that her stress level has escalated because she has no time for herself, her friends, or her husband. Indeed, she may just find that being a little restless at home wasn't so bad after all.

That said, a possible solution for the unhappy at-home mother is to find her children *one* caregiver to raise her children for the long haul—a surrogate mother, in other words. "Children need one stable adult they can depend on, and their emotional development depends more on having such a person than it does on that person being the mother," writes Hope Edelman in *Mother of My Mother.*[9] And it would be lovely, of course, if our society could count on this kind of solution for such women. As Karl Zinsmeister, editor of the *American Enterprise,* writes, "In a perfect world, there would be an abundance of intelligent, well-balanced, devoted individuals willing to attend lavishly and patiently to the demands of strangers' children—enough so that every family who wanted could have their own full-time loving surrogate."[10] Alas, this is not reality. It is extraordinarily difficult—perhaps even impossible—to find this one very special human being. And when mothers can't find her, which is most often the case, they settle for come-and-go nannies and countless day care providers. And this is *the greatest mistake a parent can make.* Indeed, this small problem of finding Johnny a home cannot be overstated: The constant merry-go-round of caregivers is enormously destructive to children. As Dr. Stanley I. Greenspan writes in *The Irreducible Needs of Children,* "The greatest fear for a child is the loss of a primary relationship."[11]

If a woman's goals in life have always rested outside the domestic arena—and surely this is the case for some women—or if the thought of raising children makes her uncomfortable because she knows she doesn't want to do the work of motherhood, then she shouldn't have children. Women must begin to give the same consideration to motherhood as they do their other career aspirations. The time to decide whether motherhood is right for us is before we get pregnant, not after. Indeed, there are many women—a growing population, actually—who choose to remain childless because they *do* take the time to think about what's involved in raising children. This is a decision worthy of great respect, far more so than those who give the issue little thought only to realize later, after they have children, that they aren't cut out to be mothers.

Because nannies and day care have become so prevalent, they appear to be safe and harmless enough. As a result, women ignore the little voice inside their heads that tells them otherwise. As one woman tells Katherine Goldman about the nanny she chose for her children, "I had a funny twinge about her when she came to us, but I was desperate, and she was good enough, I thought."[12] She was good *enough*?

Women must stop and think about what it is they're saying, what it is they're doing. They must ignore the voices around them and use common sense. Does it make sense that a baby will feel loved and appreciated if his mother leaves him every day? Does it make sense that a child won't be affected emotionally from bonding with someone and then having that person disappear—again and again? (And unless grandma is taking over, this *will* be your baby's fate.) Does it make sense that a child is going to get the same level of care in a group setting than he would one-on-one? Does it make sense that his needs will be met if there are thirty other kids whose needs also must be met—or if he has to convey his needs over and over again to a new caregiver? Does it make sense that his cognitive abilities will be fostered if he has to engage in pre-planned activities as opposed to doing what he's naturally inclined toward? Does it make sense that he will feel as though he is worthy of being heard if he has spent his entire life waiting in line? Of course not. It is inevitable that such an environment will have negative effects. The problem is that we don't always see these effects right away, so we pretend they don't exist. It's like the kitchen floor that hasn't been mopped in weeks: it doesn't look too bad at the time and seems to be holding up without a good cleaning, but it isn't until we acknowledge that it needs attention and wash it that we realize how much dirt has actually accumulated. Indeed, it could be many years before people are even aware of the damage of day care, and it can come in many forms. "Some youngsters learn not to attach themselves to any caregiver. They lose the ability to feel or express warmth, and develop a shallow and indiscriminate emotional life. Certain such children end up without any sense of personal connectedness," writes Zinsmeister.[13] And because this outcome is so difficult to quantify, many child care advocates ignore its reality. For if we cannot measure the harmful effects of substitute care ("Johnny is reading below grade level") then there must not be any harm. But there is. You just have to pay attention.

Very close attention.

Nannies

Nannies are the least common form of alternative child care—employed by only 2.4 percent of families with children below the age of five—for a very good reason: they are the most expensive. Moreover, finding a qualified nanny is like finding a needle in a haystack. If more women could afford nannies—and if finding the good ones were not so difficult—I think it's fair to assume that most families would prefer this solution to day care. The most obvious reason is that nannies can provide children with the one-on-one attention they need and deserve. Second, it is easier to have someone come to one's home than it is to drive children to a day care center every day. Third, children who are raised at home will not get sick as often as they would in day care and can live according to their own schedules and nap in the quiet and comfort of their own bedrooms.

Nevertheless, there are many hidden problems associated with hiring nannies. Perhaps the biggest shock to a new mother is the realization that nannies just don't stick around. The average mother finds herself hiring a handful of women over the years because a nanny's job is almost always temporary: most nannies will eventually seek better-paying jobs or begin families of their own. As Linda Burton discovered after her years-long search for the perfect nanny, "Many of us nanny-seekers must have acquired vastly sentimentalized notions from old English books or PBS television series that a typical nanny came to change the diapers and stayed on for weddings. The reality was that few modern-day nannies stuck around long enough to see a baby move into toddlerhood."[14] Once again, each time a mother changes providers, she causes her children great harm because *the most significant factor* in a child's development—besides a mother's influence—is having the consistent love, care, and attention of one individual throughout his or her life.

Yet even if a mother is fortunate enough to find one long-term caregiver—perhaps a family member—she will still confront a host of problems, although they, too, may not surface for several years. Her children may be not only more attached to their nanny than they are to her, but also more likely to listen to and abide by the rules of the nanny. And if the discipline style of the nanny differs from the mother's—and it almost always will—it's going to become a huge issue for the family. When this happens, a mother has to decide whether or not to change nannies. Her gut instinct will tell her that it isn't a good idea, but she also knows that her children cannot continue to receive mixed messages.

In her search for an answer, she may be unfortunate enough to come across articles like "Right Nanny, Wrong Time" in *Working Mother* magazine, which asserts that at times like these—when mothers and nannies conflict—women just have to face the fact that their children need a new nanny. "It's heart-wrenching to admit that a perfect relationship has to come to an end. We go into denial; we turn the other way when established rules begin to slide. Anything but recognize the truth."[15] The truth being, according to the article, that the mother has no choice but to switch caregivers. But the real truth is that which *Working Mother* will never tell its readers: yanking this woman from her children's lives is just about the worst thing she can do. In other words, there is no solution to this mother's problem. Which is why it's best not to hire nannies to begin with.

Mothers who hire nannies must also face the fact that their nannies know their children better than they do. Peggy Orenstein tells of one working mother who felt "just the tiniest bit threatened" by her nanny.[16] Her nanny told her that she thought one of the boys in her charge was getting too selfish; she thought he should take on more of the household chores. The mother said that at first she was put off because she felt she knew her son better than anyone. But then she realized her nanny was right. She finally admitted to herself that her nanny spent the most time with her son—over ten hours a day—so she probably knew him better than she did.

Such is the price of working motherhood.

Day Care

On October 19, 2000, Katie Couric of the *Today* show interviewed Ellen Galinsky, president of the Families and Work Institute and author of the book *Ask the Children.* The focus of the segment was whether day care could be good for children. After Galinsky told Couric how she thought day care could be a positive experience for children—helping them learn leadership skills, for example—Couric asked her whether or not she thought there were any downsides to day care. Galinsky responded hesitantly, "Well, yes, day care can be harmful." Then Couric asked her how it could be harmful, to which Galinsky responded, "Well, when it isn't good." Couric then asked her what percentage of day care centers *are* considered good, and Galinsky answered, "About 12 percent."[17]

It is important to remember that when it comes to the subject of day care, the most powerful voices in America once again prevail. Most of the information the public receives about day care is from day care *advocates.* One would have to do thorough research to find material that proves the harmful effects of day care, *not* because it doesn't exist but because it's not the side of the debate that the media wishes to provide or discuss. The public is never exposed to an honest, fair debate about day care. As Diane Fisher writes, "Academics, pediatricians, and other experts have learned to keep a prudent silence about the risks of day care, and so it is the day-care advocates—and only the advocates—we hear from on our television screens and in our parenting magazines."[18] Indeed, many women assume that because pediatricians are not crying out against day care that their silence means consent. But it doesn't. The only reason pediatricians say nothing is that if pediatricians were to speak their minds, they would lose far too many patients. So, in a way, they're stuck. It doesn't mean they think day care is good; it simply means they are forced to be political. Therefore, women should attach no significance to their silence. According to Fisher, "Many of these advocates will in private candidly concede a gap between their personal values and what they endorse professionally. But in public, you hear only the most unblinking loyalty."[19]

Which is why Ellen Galinsky cannot see the irony in her statement to Couric. She smiles and discusses how day care can be a wonderful thing for children but glosses over the fact that 88 percent of day care is either barely adequate or downright awful. Women like Galinsky dismiss such concerns and remain in thrall to the idea that day care could be great if only there were more funding. But money can never fix a system that is rife with dysfunction at its very core. And day care is absolutely dysfunctional at its very core. "America suffers a growing national epidemic of parental absence and disconnection. 'Quality' in day care cannot solve the problem. It doesn't even address it," writes Fisher.[20] Indeed, it is unreasonable for us to believe that the government has the power to make thousands of day care centers more effective. The leaders of the Family and Home Network, an organization that supports the needs of full-time mothers, expressed this point at a hearing before the U.S. House Representatives. "Seldom do 'more' and 'quality' go hand in hand. If the current child care experiences we hear about from many former and current working mothers is an accurate indication of the kind of child care most mothers are finding, then perhaps the attempt to create more day care merely hits the symptom rather than the root of the problem."[21] This makes perfect sense, doesn't it? We all know the difference between the quality of service we get at our local, privately owned grocery or hardware store and at a national food chain or Home Depot. So how is it that we believe children can be raised just as well—or even half as well—in a system that is so large, so overwhelming, that no one can possibly control its environment? Even Dr. Stanley Greenspan, author of *The Irreducible Needs of Children*, has said that America has struggled to improve day care for twenty years, without success, and that the only way it *could* be improved is for parents to provide most of their own care for their children. That way, there would be fewer people using day care and perhaps then day care could have a fighting chance. In the meantime, we have convinced ourselves that day care is harmless.

That which we desire most earnestly, we believe most easily.

On April 20, 2001, the most significant government-sponsored day care research to date was released by Dr. Jay Belsky, who first sparked debate fifteen years ago when he suggested that day care posed a risk to children of developmental problems. This new research supported his previous position. Belsky said, "We find clearly, indisputably, and unambiguously that the more time children spend in day care, the more likely they are to be aggressive and disobedient."[22] The report also found that the results are the same regardless of the type or quality of day care, the sex of the child, or whether the family is rich or poor. What matters the most, the research shows, is time: the more hours spent away from parents, the more likely children are to have behavioral problems.

Again, sounds reasonable, doesn't it? The research didn't say that the mere exposure to day care is harmful to children; it said that *exceptionally long hours* in day care is harmful. The research doesn't say that when I go to the gym and drop my daughter off in the nursery for an hour while I take an aerobics class that I'm causing her any harm, but it does point out that if I left her there all day, every day, it *would* be harmful. Nevertheless, child care advocates dispute Belsky's research. In an interview with Dan Rather, Marion Wright Edelman, president of the National Children's Defense Fund, said, "This is an opportunity not just to blame day care but to improve day care, and not to blame parents but to make it easier for parents to balance their work and family needs." When Rather asked Edelman for her response to those who would say that the research is evidence that day care just doesn't work, she replied, "Well, there's no evidence that day care just doesn't work."[23]

That which we desire most earnestly, we believe most easily.

Galinksy also questions the research—not surprisingly, since it disputes the findings in her book *Ask the Children*—by arguing that the number of hours children are away from their mothers really isn't what matters. What matters is whether a mother is stressed and tired when she returns home in the evening. If the mother is able to separate her work life from her home life, then there is no cause for concern. But who *isn't* stressed and tired after a day at the office? Moreover, it was Galinsky's organization (the Families and Work Institute) that did the research which found that it was more likely that a mother's work life would intrude on her home life, rather than the other way around.

The claims of child care advocates notwithstanding, research shows that the majority of Americans do not support day care and believe that parents are the best source of care for children. "We examined the attitudes of parents with young children, employers, and children's advocates on the issue of child care and what society should do about it. We found solid consensus on what people consider most desirable: a parent at home, either mother or father, at least for the first years of a child's life."[24] Ironically, many day care providers themselves don't support day care—not for their own children anyway. I spoke with a provider who has worked in day care for over five years. She told me that she, the director of a child care center, has let parents know that while her center provides children with the best possible care, day care is still second best. She then told me she has no intention of using day care when she has children. It is hardly surprising that child care providers would feel this way: they know best the conditions in most day care centers and how children cope in such an environment. Unfortunately, most aren't forthcoming because they need their jobs.

It is only working mothers, then, who try to prove that it is harmless for mothers to work full-time outside the home. But most of the research they gather to support their theory is questionable. There is simply no accurate, objective way to measure the evidence. Ellen Galinsky's book, *Ask the Children: What America's Children Really Think About Working Parents*, is a perfect example. It has been hailed as "groundbreaking" since it is the first book to gather information on how children feel about the fact that both of their parents work. The inference, of course, is that this somehow makes the findings more accurate, since the information comes directly from children. But Galinksy overlooks that children are blindly devoted to their mothers and are therefore unable to be objective. Moreover, they do not know any experience other than their own and hence consider their own experiences to be perfectly normal. Trying to determine how a mother's work affects children by asking the children themselves is absurd. How can we expect children to assess the sociological implications of our decisions when even we adults can't? Take, for example, Galinsky's quote from a fifteen-year-old girl whose parents both work full-time: "It's okay to work. The kid is going to turn out the same way if you work, or if you don't work."[25] This response may appease a mother's guilt, but it does not prove anything except what we, as readers, want it to prove. Just to emphasize how misinformed children are, consider this statement from an eighteen-year-old girl: "The only thing I hope I do when I am a parent is to get a career I love so everything would be easier."[26] There you have it: we've somehow managed to teach young girls that "getting a career" when they become mothers will help make life *easier* for them.

Working mothers and child care advocates are also quick to point out that many children whose parents both worked "turned out fine." While this can certainly be true, it is once again impossible to gather the kind of information one would need in order to determine whether or not a person "turned out fine." There is simply no concrete way to measure this. What do we mean when we say a person "turned out fine"? Are we referring to whether someone can hold down a job or is happily married? How do you measure how much baggage a person has? As Greenspan writes, "It's difficult to measure many of the most important emotional capacities, such as intimacy, sense of self, and future capacities to parent and nurture children."[27] Besides, adult children are no less loyal to their mothers than young children are, so again their analysis is not objective. Suffice it to say that trying to determine whether a child "turns out fine" is very difficult: there are just too many variables. This is why it is important that women begin to listen to their instincts—and their guilt—and use good, old-fashioned common sense when it comes to children and day care. Working mothers have been given far too much credit for the one thing they know the least about: children. Women must begin to turn a deaf ear to those who, because of a need to justify their decision to work, create questionable theories about what children need.

Some, for instance, claim day care teaches children independence. "Children [in high-quality day care] are stronger leaders, more independent and more self-confident," says day care provider Bobbie Noonan.[28] This is blatantly false. First of all, there is no such thing as an independent baby. Babies are completely and totally *de*pendent, and they stay this way for some time. Thrusting a baby into day care will never create the independent nature working mothers are looking for: "To develop into an emotionally healthy person, your child needs to progress through the stages gradually. Moving from dependency to being able to do things independently is challenging, and requires your patience and support."[29] In other words, parents must first meet their babies' need for *de*pendence before they can even think about a child becoming independent. As William and Wendy Dreskin, former child care directors and authors of *The Day Care Decision*, write, "Children who are nourished by love feel secure and have the easiest time when the 'famine' of separation hits. But children who have been deprived since infancy have no reserves to fall back on."

Indeed, this has been known for some time. In 1962, the U.S. Department of Health, Education, and Welfare's Office of Child Development published a booklet entitled "Your Child From 1 to 6." In the section on babies and toddlers, it reads:

> If [the toddler] continues to receive the warm assurance he has had, he will grow more sure of himself. If he is pushed out faster than he is ready to go, he will always be a little less confident, and a little more dependent on others than he might otherwise have been. These early experiences have a lifelong effect. Even though the child doesn't remember what actually happened, and lacks words to give it shape in his mind, the feelings remain. He learns that he can count on people—or that he cannot; that he will be allowed to try things out—or that he'll be constantly thwarted. These characteristic ways of looking at things tend to persist and become a fixed part of the personality.

In reality, then, day care actually produces the opposite of the effect that child care advocates claim. Developing independence, or even overcoming shyness, can never be remedied by putting one's child in day care because that type of environment is not how children gain a sense of self. Furthermore, what child-care advocates call independence, you and I might see as something else. As Jeree Pawl, director of the infant-parent program at the University of California-San Francisco said, "In most day care centers, it's a pecking order; it's like a bunch of wild chickens in a hen yard."[30] The result is that "the loudest and most obnoxious behavior is what gets rewarded with attention from overloaded adult caretakers and intimidated peers," writes Karl Zinsmeister.[31] Indeed, a child can become independent in any number of ways, but how this trait manifests itself in a child's personality is key. As Linda Burton points out, "It is the quality of a child's independence that concerns most mothers: Was it born of necessity or self-confidence? Do their children know they can make it on their own because they're rich in resources or because, by golly, they had to? Can they help other people along the way because somebody took the time to help them or do they ignore the needs of other people because no one was there when they had a need? Will they be able to combat any potential challenges because they feel nurtured, secure in themselves and their abilities or because they had to fight to get it?"[32] Independence, then—as much as we revere it—is not always a good quality. Indeed, I have known several people whose independent natures made a relationship with them extraordinarily difficult, even impossible.

Another favorite rationalization is the idea that babies need day care in order to be intellectually stimulated. Many women believe that babies require stimulation that their mothers can't provide. But not only is this clinically false, it is silly. One working mother tells Betty Holcomb, "Day care turned out to be an enriching experience for me and my son. At ten weeks old, he was coming home with artwork."[33] Unfortunately, too many mothers are unaware that the single greatest factor in the life of a newborn is emotional attachment. Not only is intellectual development secondary, it is practically irrelevant. As Fisher writes, "We must remember that it is the *emotional* development of the infant that forms the foundation upon which all later achievements are based. For the infant, a mother is the environment—pre-natally and post-natally. As a society, we are uncomfortable admitting this—but it is a biological fact."[34] In other words, trying to develop a baby's intellect with the help of specially designed toys or creative projects is useless. The ordinary kitchen utensils in our cupboards are much more likely to engage babies than anything we can buy for them at Toys 'R Us. Babies just do not develop intellectually in the way older children do. They learn and grow by watching their mothers day in and day out, since repetition is the one thing that truly does help foster their intellect.

And then, of course, there's the issue of socialization. Obviously children want and need socialization. The question is when and in what form they need it. Babies, for example, do not socialize. Even new moms are aware that the playgroups they join are for *them* (as it should be), not for their newborns. It isn't until children are older—around two years old—that they begin to engage in parallel play with other children. And even then it isn't necessary; it's just fun. It only becomes necessary around the age of three. Unfortunately, today we've decided that day care is the only means for socialization—as if before there was day care, children were bored and lonely. But let us not forget that before there was day care, there were moms at home—and lots of them. Neighborhoods were our children's means of socialization, and if mothers hadn't decided to flee their homes, neighborhoods would still be the best means for interaction. While it is true that our neighborhoods are no longer what they once were, there are still plenty of other activities that children can get involved in—playgroups, storytime, Moms Day Out—in order for children to have interaction with other children. Day care is not the answer.

I am reminded of a baby shower I attended. As we all know, baby showers comprise two generations of women: the friends of the woman who's having a baby—usually in their twenties or thirties—and the friends of her mother. At this particular shower, the younger set was mostly made up of working mothers, while the older set had, of course, been home with their children. I remember two distinct conversations, one with the younger set and one with the older set. In the conversation of working mothers, an attorney with a three-year-old daughter in day care told us that she was in the middle of a job change. She said she had been laid off from her job and was currently collecting unemployment. When another mother asked her about how things were going at home with her daughter, she replied confidently that her daughter was still in day care. She said she's working on various projects at home and really "loves her daughter's day care center because it provides her with great stimulation." She adds, "There's just no way I could provide her with the stimulation she needs."

Fast forward about an hour. I was sitting at a table with the older generation, and one of the mothers told a story about her daughter's having run away when she was six years old because she was convinced that her mother was the worst mother in the world. So she packed her bags, winter coat and all—though it was only summertime—and took off down the street. The woman told us that she knew where her daughter was headed, so she called her neighbor whose daughter was the same age as her own. While she was on the phone, she heard her daughter stomp into the neighbor's house crying, telling her friend how mean her mother was and wondering if she could live there with them. The two mothers hung up, and the neighbor told the girl that, yes, certainly she could live with them. She said they had room in the basement with a very comfortable bed and bath. The girl was very happy and proceeded to unpack her belongings. Then the mother handed the girl a dust cloth and told her she'd have to earn her keep by helping the mother clean the house every day. In less than half an hour, the girl was on her way home. It seems her mother wasn't so bad after all. As I sat there listening to this woman's story, I thought about days long gone: when mothers were at home, enjoying every delightful bit of their children's nonsense—and about how women were around to help each other out. Then I thought of the attorney and wondered if she had any idea what she was giving up.

The rationalizations of working mothers have no end. One woman tells Arlie Hochschild that her son Nicky is in day care from eight in the morning to five in the evening every day, but since she likes to work out at the gym twice a week, she makes sure to have her husband or sister pick him up for her so that he doesn't have to stay at day care until six. After all, she says, "I don't see why some parents *have* kids if they don't want to take care of them." Here's a woman who honestly believes she is a better mother because she refuses to let her son stay in day care one extra hour twice a week. In her mind, *five* nine-hour days—forty-five hours a week—seems reasonable. But forty-seven hours just wouldn't be right.

Others maintain that there is no difference between a child who is raised at home and a child who is raised in day care *as long as* Mom is a "sensitive, responsive, and caring parent" during the time she does spend with her children, says Holcomb.[35] That's like saying there's no difference between an employee who comes to work every day and does the job and an employee who only shows up one day a week, but on that particular day is really nice. The truth is, "young children do not form a strong attachment to a person they see little of, no matter how kindly the person is or how superlative the quality of time spent together," write William and Wendy Dreskin. Indeed, Holcomb might as well tell mothers that raising their children is a waste of time. One full-time mother addresses this point online to family therapist Gayle Peterson. The mother writes that she is frustrated with the media reports that say it doesn't matter whether she is home with her children: "How can it be that children are not negatively affected when they only see their parents two hours each day?"[36] The answer Peterson gives is the standard feel good response: that, ultimately, whatever works best for this mother is what matters the most. Peterson implies, however, that working motherhood is ultimately beneficial to everyone because "no child benefits from a mother who never develops any interests or activities outside of her children"[37] (as though being employed is the only way to pursue one's interests and talents). Still, Peterson is quick to add that this mother should not devalue the work she does at home because "it is priceless."[38]

The problem with Peterson's response (typical of working mothers and child-care advocates) is that it's contradictory. You simply can't say in one breath that there's no difference between the child who is raised at home and the child who is not *and* that full-time motherhood is "priceless." If mothering is "priceless," such an important job that one can't put a price on it, how can it make little difference whether mothers stay home and perform this work? Indeed, Peterson doesn't answer the woman's question at all. Instead, she dances around it, using politically correct jargon to evade the fact that the woman is right: of course there's a difference between a child who is raised at home and a child who is raised in day care.

A final rationalization, which I believe is rather innocent, stemming mainly from ignorance, is the claim that children "just *love* day care," that they can't wait to get there and never want to leave. This enthusiasm isn't something for mothers to get excited about. For one thing, a child's unwillingness to go home with his mother at the end of the day is not good. Second, what these mothers do not appreciate is that children are attracted to what they know, for they have nothing with which to compare their experience. If a child has always been in day care, then day care is where the child is most comfortable. Day care *is* home, so of course they want to be there. The point is that it's not our children's job to know what's good for them; it's our job as their parents. A child may love (or say he loves) day care, but he also loves candy. Does this mean we should let him eat it all day, every day? Children also don't think they're tired when they really are (which is why their initial reaction to naptime and bedtime is a resounding "No!"). Should we let them stay up? No, because we know they are tired even though they don't think they are. We know that once their heads hit the pillow, they'll be asleep. That's why we're the parents and they're the children. It makes no sense to think that because children appear to love day care that there is no harm done. "Children will become reconciled to their fate. They may stop expressing themselves to the day care workers and their parents, but their feelings have not evaporated. Once children have realized that complaints in any form consistently bring censure, even if they are directly questioned they will dutifully repeat that they like day care," write the Dreskins.[39]

A common misperception of working mothers and child-care advocates is that they assume all full-time mothers think their children should never be separated from them. But this just isn't true. Most full-time moms agree that it is healthy for them and their children to have a break from one another. The real issue is a matter of *how long* and *how often* children should be away from their mothers (which is why Belsky's research makes perfect sense). Many full-time moms use their local Moms Day Out program, for example, which is designed to give parents a break and give their children a chance to explore the world without them. Many mothers also use the nursery at their local gym. These settings bear a striking resemblance to day care. The difference is in the amount of time children spend there: an average of perhaps five hours a week. This is just enough time to make up for the socialization that is lacking in our neighborhoods, but not enough to cause any real damage. The working mother debate, then, is not about whether mothers and children should ever be apart, but whether mothers are using child care resources in a responsible fashion. It's about whether women view their role as mothers as their priority and focus on their own needs as time allows, or whether they view their own needs as their priority and focus on their children as time allows.

The most powerful voices in America have an obligation to warn parents of the detriments of day care, and they aren't doing it. Instead, they talk about how day care has the potential to be good one day and offer suggestions about how mothers can improve the quality of care their children are receiving, as though working mothers have any control over what happens when they are not around. Here's Ellen Galinsky's suggestion: "There's always something you can do. Maybe just bring a book to a provider so she can read to your child. Say something that makes her more interested in her job. If we want better for our children, change is not going to be handed to us. We have to make it happen."[40] Instead of women getting the message that the only way to ensure that their children will get the best possible care is to raise them at home, they get the message that they can help their children get what they need by trying to alter the emotional outlook of their children's transient day care provider.

That which we desire most earnestly, we believe most easily.

No reasonable person believes that day care shouldn't exist at all. But day care was initially begun as a Head Start program designed to help low-income families by providing a place for them to keep their children safe while the parents went to work. No one thought to argue that such an environment was preferable to the home; it was simply supposed to be a safe alternative for mothers who had no choice but to work. But the day care today has little to do with this initial plan for alternative child care. Today's day care is open to anyone who wants it. Indeed, we have come to believe that the government should provide every family with this option. Day care, then, has become our right— rather than a last resort for those who have exhausted every other means to care for their children. As Karl Zinsmeister observes, "there's a difference between a compromise made in reaction to some crisis of fate and an arrangement made simply because one wants to maximize one's own position while ignoring serious costs to others."[41]

It is disturbing that we have become so used to day care that we do not appreciate that mothers are our most vital resource. Children do not raise themselves, and they do not "thrive" in day care. They just get used to it. Children will get used to anything we ask them to; this is why our power is so frightening. And it is the reason we have a responsibility not to ask our children to get used to anyone but us. Regardless of how a working mother explains to her children her reasons for being gone all day, the only thing her children will take from her explanation is that there's someplace else she would rather be.

～

"I Have It All Planned Out."

I had it all planned out: I'd birth Ruby, bond with her, and then resume life as I knew it, writing, working, reading, going to movies and restaurants. Ruby would be nearby, strapped on to me like some exotic appendage, delightful, lovely, and obedient, living *my life* with *me*.

And then, one June, Ruby came.

Laurie Wagner

SOCIETY'S REFUSAL TO ACKNOWLEDGE THE TRUTH about what's involved in raising children has only fueled the working mother debate. While it is true that no woman can appreciate what it's like to have children until she has children of her own, the fact remains that motherhood is an even greater shock for today's woman. We have been groomed for a life at the office, not for a life at home. Having children is often the last thing on young women's minds, and while postponing motherhood has its advantages, one cannot deny the disadvantages. In addition to the biological implications, all the years women spend focused on themselves and their careers makes for a much more difficult adjustment when they finally do settle down. Women get used to living an easy, predictable life, one in which everything fits into a nice, tidy routine. Waking up to motherhood is a shock.

I remember a conversation I had with a friend of mine who, at the time, was not yet a mother. She and her husband had been together for over ten years and married for two. She told me about her recent trips to Israel and Paris and said she would be taking about four more trips over the next several months. I told her how great it sounded and felt certain the conversation would eventually find its way to motherhood.

"I guess I have to get all these trips in before I have kids," she said, "I mean, there's just no way to go anywhere after that, is there?"

"Well, basically," I answered.

"But you're lucky to have your mother close by so you and your husband can get away."

"Yes," I said, "but the trips are shorter and not quite as extravagant as Paris—more like weekend binges in Chicago or New York."

"Yeah, that's true. By the way, remember my friend Sara? She just had her second baby. I can't believe I haven't seen her in seven months."

After a pause, she added, "I don't know what it is. People just change after they have kids. They don't go out; and whenever I ask them how they're doing, they tell me all these things about motherhood that make it sound so . . . negative."

"What do you mean?" I asked.

"Well, like they say to me, 'Everything changes when you have children,' or 'We don't get out as much.'"

My friend went on to say that she couldn't imagine her life without children, but that she was pretty sure she could wait to have her life change so drastically. She has always wanted kids, she said, but having lived motherhood somewhat vicariously—through the lives of her mom friends—makes her wonder whether she's ready for that life. For the first time, she told me, she had considered what her life could be like if she chose not to have children.

It cannot be overstated: Motherhood changes everything.

Everything.

When we become mothers, it's as though we've stepped off a plane and entered a foreign country. To make matters worse, society grossly understates how dramatically women's lives change as a result of having children. Women can find reams of information about pregnancy and baby care, but there are few books that discuss the truth about motherhood. *The Mask of Motherhood* by Susan Maushart is one exception. Maushart writes that mothers wear masks designed to "disguise the chaos and complexity of our lived experience." These masks "keep women from speaking clearly what they know, and from hearing truths too threatening to face. That for every woman who blooms in pregnancy there's another who develops root rot. That the persistent cry of a newborn can make your husband's snoring sound like a sonata. That your child's physical demands will diminish at only a fraction of the rate at which her emotional ones will multiply and intensify. That getting the knack of combining motherhood with career is like getting the knack of brain surgery: nice work if you can get it, but 99.9% of us never will."[1] This silence—these masks—is one of the reasons women assume they can give birth and then go about their business as though children would conform to their lives rather than the other way around.

It's not that women don't realize their lives will change when they become mothers, it's that they do not understand exactly *how* their lives will change. They've heard that raising children is hard work—but they don't know what it is *specifically* that makes it so hard. They are aware that they will have to make sacrifices—remember, this is the reason they wait to have children—but they do not realize the *extent* of their sacrifices. And while it is true that no woman can be totally prepared for motherhood, it is much harder for today's women who have little experience with children and don't even entertain the idea of being home with them. When they finally do become mothers, they have a kind of epiphany. "Being a mom is just a million times harder than negotiating a real estate contract or writing a hit song or studying for a physics test. It's a lot harder than anything I've ever done in my life. And nobody tells you that," says Bernie Nash.[2]

There are two reasons women like Nash feel shortchanged. The first is that there are very few books that deal with the realities of motherhood, and the second is that the media won't even discuss traditional motherhood, much less give us any details. And quite frankly, they can't. For while we are watching a much-loved media personality on television, somewhere out there is a well-paid nanny who is doing the work of motherhood for her. We'd be better off asking the nanny about the realities of motherhood.

Or, better yet, keep reading. For I have outlined below the four aspects of motherhood that I believe affect a woman's life the most, which no one bothers to mention. Some are more pleasant than others and may make you rethink whether you even want children. But, then, that's the point. Because if you don't go into motherhood with your eyes wide open, believe me, you will wish you had. You will wish someone had told you what you can really expect. Though motherhood is not the pretty picture you see on television or that you read about in books. It is extremely challenging work. But it is still the most powerful, important, gratifying, beautiful journey a woman can take.

Falling in Love

Perhaps the most shocking discovery for today's women is when they find out how instinctive their desire to mother is—and how in love they are with their babies. Sounds rather obvious, doesn't it? But it's not. When was the last time you read an article or heard the news media talk about how becoming a mother causes a woman to love someone else so intensely that she finds herself caring very little about anything else? The reason you don't hear this is that it goes against everything the women's movement has been trying to prove. I remember watching an interview with Valerie Bertinelli on Lifetime several years ago. Bertinelli had put her acting career on the back burner when she became a mother, and the interviewer asked her how she felt her life had changed as a result of becoming a mother, how it was different from her previous life. Bertinelli answered, "What life? I don't remember my life before I had my son. Whatever it was, it didn't matter."[3] This from a woman whose previous life was far from banal. I think the reason I remember this interview is that I thought it was so unusual—and so wonderful—that a celebrity like Bertinelli would not only leave the limelight to raise her son but that she could talk about the experience of having children as though she were any one of us.

Which, of course, she is. And that's the point.

But Bertinelli is rare, for most high-profile women are consumed with thoughts of pregnancy, maternity leave, and day care. Never do the media discuss the fact that many women don't *want* to return to their former lives, as though something huge, something monumental, hasn't just taken place. Never do the media warn women that they won't be able to focus on their work the way they did before they became mothers, because they will be too preoccupied with thoughts of their babies. Not only do mothers worry about the care their babies are receiving in their absence, they miss them terribly. That's what happened to a woman I met who was in the midst of quitting her job as a nurse in the Navy to become a full-time mom. Her "baby" was over a year old at the time, and I asked her what had changed her mind. She said, "I just want to be with him. I got to thinking, What's the point of having children in the first place?" After telling her about my book, I asked her if she would mind sharing with me why she hadn't thought she might feel this way beforehand. She said that it never occurred to her to *not* go back to work (a clear indication of the times we live in).

There was a day care center right across the street from where she worked, so she assumed everything would work out great. "But," she said, "no one ever told me how much I would miss him."

Indeed, and that's because society refuses to acknowledge the intense emotions that accompany motherhood, for the idea of talking about loving your baby so much that all you want to do is take care of him is practically taboo. Recognizing this would undo all the hard work of the women's movement, because putting oneself first is paramount to their platform. Putting children first is considered beneath us as women. But loving her child more than herself does not lower a woman's status, it raises it. Motherhood elevates women, which is one of the intrinsic rewards of sacrifice. A stronger society would recognize this.

Shift in Values

Some have said that people don't really grow up until they have children, the idea being that taking on the responsibility of raising a family forces us to shift the focus away from ourselves to others for the first time in our lives. It allows us to see the world in a different light. As my husband says, "Having children is like putting on a new pair of glasses." There is no question about it: becoming a parent causes a monumental shift in one's values. In this way, then, one might say that having children marks the beginning of our lives. Unfortunately, the current generation talks about waiting to have children as though the event will mark the end of their lives. What they mean to say, of course, is that they won't be able to go away for the weekend or go to the movies on the spur of the moment, because they'll be "stuck" at home with children. But it isn't until they take the plunge that they realize how wrong they were to view parenthood in this way. For while it is true that spontaneity is no longer a part of our lives, the shift in values that parenthood brings, this new way of looking at the world, is so gratifying and so powerful that we can't even believe we used to attach so much significance to the idea of being able to get up and go.

This is a relatively new phenomenon. In previous generations, men and women did view family life as the beginning rather than the end of their lives. Because of this, they had a much healthier attitude toward family life. We view family life as something to be postponed, something to worry about later, even something that gets in the way of our plans. In 1995, my mother attended her graduate school reunion at Radcliffe. One of the female professors who gave a lecture about careers and motherhood told the group that women would need to deal with children as an "intrusion" in their lives. In viewing family this way, it makes sense that today's mothers are struck by their newfound sense of responsibility. Many are surprised to discover that what they thought was important before they had a child seems utterly irrelevant afterward. And this is exactly what marks the change in a woman's value system, a change that becomes amplified over the years.

The First Year of Motherhood

Despite falling in love with our babies and growing up a bit in our view of the world, we find, admittedly, some aspects of motherhood very difficult. Most people don't talk about the unpleasant realities of motherhood because they think they aren't supposed to; or, if they're from the old school, they believe that there are some things in life that you just don't talk about.

I disagree. In fact, this is one area where I believe my generation has the upper hand. While there is much to be said for modesty, holding back truth is ultimately counterproductive. And nowhere is this more true than when women bring their babies home for the first time. So here's the truth: Life at home with a baby—even beyond the newborn stage—can be difficult. Extremely difficult. You may think you'll be exempt from experiencing any hardship, and I hope that you don't experience anything other than sheer bliss. But you will. I know you have a husband who has come into the twenty-first century and plans to share everything with you (I discuss this further in the next section), but here's the shocker: this doesn't mean much when it comes to parenting a newborn. Furthermore, you probably wonder what could be so hard about babies. *Don't they just sleep a lot?* I remember talking to a friend shortly after I had my baby. She was thirty-five, pregnant for the first time, and had begun her search for the perfect nanny. She said, "I know it's going to be hard to find someone good, but it's not like babies require that much work. They just sleep most of the time."

It is true that babies sleep a lot. In fact, as they get older, mothers may wish for the periods of time they had to rest when their children were babies. But to suggest that babies are easy to care for because they sleep a lot only serves to fuel a mother's grandiose plans to return to the workforce. Women cannot comprehend the unpredictable nature of babies. A mother whose baby is colicky, for example, is going to find babies far more challenging than those whose babies merely "hang-out" and look cute, as my friend Lee's baby did. Women may know that they won't get a lot of sleep at first, but they cannot understand how this lack of sleep will manifest itself. They presume they'll just "sleep when the baby sleeps," because that's what people tell them to do, but it isn't that simple. When a newborn sleeps, it's like a one or two-hour gift from God. It's heaven-sent. So it's hard to just go to sleep—even though you're dying to do so—when you're craving a moment to yourself, when you still have to contend with your breasts, get something to eat, go to the bathroom, and take a shower. It's hard to go to sleep when you are thinking about an errand you need to run but can't—and how confining that feels. It's hard to sleep in one-hour intervals throughout the day and night when all of your life you have been used to sleeping for eight hours and being awake for sixteen.

And it's not just the sleep issue. Many new mothers don't feel comfortable in their new surroundings, what with sitting in a chair breastfeeding all day and night. *All* day and night. Actually, that part might not be so bad (it is short-lived, after all) if your baby were content to just latch on to your breast and look at you lovingly while he sucks away, but it doesn't always work that way. Indeed, I found breastfeeding my daughter to be a terrible ordeal (neither she nor I was happy until I finally substituted a bottle for my breast—three excruciating weeks later), and the manner in which my beautiful new baby would cry every moment she was not on my breast was almost intolerable. Of course, this was just my experience; I don't mean to suggest that it will necessarily be yours. It probably won't.

But it could.

And while breastfeeding may work out better for you than it did for me, there is less chance that you will escape the crying. And let me tell you, there's crying—and then there's crying. My daughter cried for many months. At the time we thought it was colic, and then I realized that colic is just a nice term pediatricians came up so they wouldn't have to tell mothers that some babies are just more difficult than others. I remember a friend of mine (also a new mom at the time) happened to be at my house when my daughter had one of her spells just before naptime, and her eyes almost popped out of her head. "Is *that* what you've been talking about?" she asked. "Oh, my God." It seems her son never cried to the point where he would choke or throw up or act as though there were needles stuck in his head.

But there's more. Bringing a baby home also causes emotional turmoil, as you get tossed between a love so deep you think you might actually burst and a sheer annoyance of your baby's existence because you're sleep deprived and don't know what you're feeling or saying half the time. If your baby cries more than usual (not that you have any idea what *usual* is when you're a new parent), marital conflict may follow as you and your husband start telling each other how stupid the other one is to think that whatever he or she is doing is going to make the baby stop crying. Furthermore, you can kiss good-bye the sex you thought you would have immediately after your episiotomy healed. In fact, you can kiss sex goodbye for quite a while, at least the sex you once knew.

For most of us, it's the sacrifices that are so overwhelming. There's simply no way to describe what it's like to never again wake up in the morning to the quiet and comfort of your own thoughts and a hot cup of coffee. Indeed, women are thrust into a world where they are expected to forget their physical and emotional needs. They must rise early in the morning—seven days a week—(say good-bye to late-night partying) and often forgo the immediate cup of coffee or shower to which they've become accustomed. They must be on call around the clock, ignoring their need for hunger or sleep while they tend to matters that cannot wait. They work with an appendage attached to them wherever they go—even when they visit the bathroom. They do not sleep for months. Their breasts or no longer their own (and they're certainly no longer their husbands'), and they will only be able to run one errand a day—if that. Once a mother adjusts to her new life, she will have to be creative in penciling in time for herself because it will not exist otherwise. Suffice it to say, those first few months at home aren't always a blissfully happy time.

Men, Marriage, and Motherhood

It is this last secret—shock, really—about motherhood that women need to be concerned about. It's the secret no one, not even your mother, told you. Once you have children, your marriage will never again be the same. You can forget romance and passion and all that stuff about happily ever after, at least in the way you envisioned it.

I do not mean to be negative. People can be happily married only if they let go of the idea that marriage is supposed to "complete" them and if they shift their view of what constitutes a healthy marriage. Marriage has little to do with finding a soul mate. Indeed, marriage is a far more practical endeavor than we wish it were. We *wish* it were about passion and romance and happily ever after, but in fact marriage has more to do with mutual respect, shared values, and commitment. Furthermore, marriage was originally designed for procreation; and while we are far more progressive in our thinking today, we are foolish to think that this isn't still a reason for marriage. "It's no exaggeration to say that marriage is about children. It always has been—although we in the industrialized west have in the last hundred years or so persuaded ourselves otherwise. Marriage, we now insist, is about romantic love," writes Susan Maushart in *Wifework*.[4] Clearly, then, marriage is more about being parents together than it is about being a couple. So it makes perfect sense that our marriages won't stay the same after we have children.

The problem is accepting this. And part of the reason we don't is that those of us in my generation desperately want marriage to be something it is not. Deep down, we want marriage to be more about passion and romance than about practicality and family life. We don't think of marriage as a long-term commitment, since we can get divorced at the drop of a hat. It's not that we don't want our marriages to last forever, but we have no idea what is needed to make this happen. We have not been taught the things that people in previous generations were taught to think about when they married: money, values, in-laws ("When you marry, you marry the family"), goals, priorities, religious background, and children. If we have major philosophical differences with the man or woman we love, we believe we can work them out: love will see us though. Or better yet, maybe we can change our spouse. But love is not enough to make a marriage work. As Pepper Schwartz writes in an article entitled "Love Is Not All You Need," "Making a commitment based on hormone-addled logic is a recipe for disappointment, if not disaster."[5] Even Oprah and her psychological gurus have been telling us this for years now.

One of the reasons for the high divorce rate is that we have grown up believing that men and women are essentially the same. The idea of equality has been instilled in us throughout our lives, often in ways of which we aren't even conscious. I remember listening to one of my local talk radio personalities, who happens to be around my age (mid-thirties). He was discussing a book that had just been released, by a woman who espoused the idea that men should have the ultimate say in marriage. (Not *The Surrendered Wife*, but in that same vein.) He said that today's generation has a hard time thinking along these lines—himself included—for the simple reason that we have grown up having the notion of equality drilled into our heads. Asking an entire generation to think differently, as the author of this book does—particularly when we believe our point of view to be an example of genuine progress—is almost impossible.

The idea that men and women should approach parenting similarly, that men and women are simply interchangeable is, next to the idea of having it all, the most bogus aspect of modern-day feminism. For no matter how enlightened today's husbands may be, no matter how good they are in the delivery room or how many diapers they are willing to change, women can count on the fact that fathers will never be parents *in the same way* mothers are. As Maushart writes, "There is nothing shocking about the finding that mothers and fathers inhabit substantially different worlds; they have done so for all of human history. The shock is that we thought we were going to be different. We were wrong."[6] Indeed, for all of our attempts at making marriage more equitable—and, admittedly, there has been significant improvement—there remain some inherent differences between men and women that will never change.

Never.

And there's a very good reason why: nature. Unfortunately, feminists have done a superb job of trying to weed out this fact of life. Men and women really aren't that different, say the most ardent feminists; they've just been socialized to think they are. These women also do not accept that the differences between men and women become amplified when a couple has children. But they do, and denying this doesn't make it go away. Michael Gurian discusses these biological differences in *The

Wonder of Girls. When it comes to parenthood, Gurian writes, a man "does not experience the hormonal, biochemical bond with his children that his wife does. His bond will mainly be social and psychological. It is a bond of a different quality and not to note this is to rob the mother of the special quality of her bond with her offspring."[7] No matter how egalitarian a couple's relationship is prior to having children, there is no question that this dynamic changes the moment they become parents. "If the lines between what is expected and what happens in the real world have always been fuzzy, rarely have they been more so than when men and women consider what life will be like as parents together after the birth of a baby," writes Nordin.[8]

This was a reality that people in previous generations understood. Women didn't have the same expectations for marital fulfillment that they do today. Both women and men today give very little thought to what it means to be married, partly because they never been told what to expect and partly because they don't give the future much thought at all. They have grown up thinking only about the here and now. Look at our obsession with weddings, now ridiculously inflated. Women focus an inordinate amount of time and energy on their Big Day. It's all about money, fun, and fashion, but when the exictement is over, the couple may find that they were living a fantasy. Is it any wonder, then, that the divorce rate has skyrocketed? Midge Decter writes that today's generation of women has too big of a burden to shoulder: the idea that they should "assume the responsibility for providing themselves with something that could be adjudged a rich and fulfilling life."[9] And marital happiness is one of the responsibilities we have taken on.

Of course, we all want to be happily married—and we can be. But we won't be if we're always searching for complete fulfillment in marriage. It isn't realistic to expect that one person can fulfill all our needs. This is why it is healthy to have friends. Too many people, when they learn that their spouse is not all they had hoped or expected, think they can find happines elsewhere, but they can't. As Diane Sollee, founder and director of the Coalition for Marriage, Family, and

Couples Education, writes, "We need to recognize that every happy, successful couple has approximately ten areas of disagreement that they will never resolve. If we switch partners, we'll just get ten new areas of disagreement."[10] Part of the reason the divorce rate is so high is that people do not want to deal with the unpleasant realities of married life. They want marriage to be something it is not. At some point, we are going to have to learn to accept that marriage and family is not about excitement, passion, and dreams, but about commitment and responsibility. This doesn't mean that there aren't moments in which marriage can be exciting or passionate; it just means that such moments may be few. Indeed, the true richness of marriage comes not from spontaneity or fantasy but from a sense of place, an inner peace and security that can only be found in a family.

It makes sense, then, that marriage is not about finding a soul mate but about finding someone with whom we have a shared vision. It is about finding someone who has the same values that we do and who views family as the priority if we plan on having children. In our parents' day, loving one's spouse and wanting fulfillment from marriage were no less important, it just wasn't viewed with the same intensity as it is today. Fading romance amidst the pressures of raising a family did not catapult women into a marital crisis. It was simply understood that this was the stuff of married life. Today we do not expect to have to make concessions, or sacrifices, when we marry. Instead we think of marriage as a means of self-fulfillment: *our* careers, *our* money, *our* goals, *our* needs, *our* wants, *our* plans for the future. We don't want to believe that getting married will change these plans. But it does. This is the reason marriage is so difficult. And it is the reason why we better be good and ready to settle down when we decide to take the plunge.

It isn't surprising, then, that when today's women become mothers and problems begin to surface, they find themselves overwhelmed. *It wasn't supposed to be like this! No one ever told me that marriage and motherhood was so much work!* If women find themselves having less sex—or fewer three-hour conversations about the meaning of life—they begin to worry. They assume their marriages are in trouble when, in truth, the stagnation is perfectly natural. Lisa Wolfe, mother of two, writes in *O* about her and her husband's return after a trip to Venice, a trip that was designed to elicit some of that pre-parent marital bliss. She writes, "One night when I am washing my face before bed, Joe grabs my waist and we kiss. But then our older son gets an ear infection and wakes up screaming, and our younger son catches it and wakes up screaming, and before we know it we're so exhausted we revert to our pre-Venice ways."[11] Welcome to parenthood. My generation is shocked to find that marriage is nothing like what we thought it would be. The problems that have always existed in marriage—money, kids, housework, sex, religion, in-laws—are still a part of marriage, no matter how liberated we think we are. And if we don't begin to accept this, we will never learn how to be happily married.

Of all the causes of marital strife, the issue of men's and women's roles remains the most common. Part of the reason for this is that household chores and child care are things that couples are forced to contend with daily. The conversations are always the same. First the wife says, "I suppose you think this is my job? Why am I the only one cooking and doing laundry around here? Did it ever occur to you that you have two hands?" Then the husband comes back with, "I don't see you mowing the lawn or taking out the trash or fixing the kitchen sink." Then the wife says, "Oh, please, it's not like those things have to be done every day."

And on and on it goes.

Many women today enter into marriage believing that women's liberation has ensured they will never face the same type of gender issues that their parents did. And in some ways, they are right: gender roles are no longer set in stone. Perhaps the most obvious change is that women are no longer expected to serve their men, nor do men want them to. Fathers can now be seen changing diapers, cleaning kitchens, and toting their babies around in Snuglies. These are all good things. But our search for gender equality dismisses the biological differences between men and women, differences that become undeniably magnified once children arrive. Women's liberation has given men and women the impression that our marriages will be—and should be—equal. Not the kind of equal that it makes sense to expect, the kind where each partner gives more than his or her share at different points so that one person doesn't end up with all the responsibilities, but the kind in which each partner is responsible for everything: producing an income, raising the children, and taking care of the household. But this philosophy has failed. For one thing, it doesn't make sense from a practical standpoint, as any good partnership requires a division of labor. Second, it makes no allowances for gender, particularly when it comes to child care. And this just isn't realistic.

Nothing is ever equal when you're married; that's what makes marriage so challenging. While I have no complaints about the division of labor in our household (my husband is very self-sufficient, respectful of communal space, and does dishes and laundry), I still manage to do more around the house than he does. And while this may be the norm in most households, the reason for it isn't always what people presume. Gender feminists like to argue that any time we see a family in which the woman does more around the house than the man, it's because of discrimination, because men have still not taken responsibility for their share of the labor (child care included). This is the case in some households, but more often than not, the reason for the unfair division of labor has to do with time. Indeed, you would have a hard time finding a man today who will tell you that he thinks child care and household tasks are "women's work." You will, on the other hand, find him saying that he has so little time at home that to spend it cooking and cleaning when he needs and wants to be with his children makes little sense.

Unfortunately, this is a fact of life that is never taken into consideration by gender feminists. In 2002, Gloria Steinem told Oprah that America has come a long way with respect to equality but said, as one would expect her to, that we "still have more work to do." She said that even though many marriages today start off on an equal footing, everything changes once the children come. Despite our progress, she says, we are ultimately still left with inequality. Betty Friedan agrees. But isn't it possible that if we *have* made so much progress, as Steinem and Freidan concede we have, and yet still struggle with gender roles, that there just may be some biological reason for this?

Gurian thinks so. He accuses "selective feminism" of ignoring the basic biological differences between boys and girls and argues that this does a great disservice to society by forcing us to pretend as though these differences don't matter. For example, he talks about how the female brain secretes more serotonin than a male's, which directly relates to impulse control. (Think men and sex.) He also writes that females secrete more oxytocin, which relates to the interest in playing with "care objects" or with babies. (Which is exactly why my daughter will find any inanimate object and pretend it's a baby so she can cradle it, rock it to sleep, and change its diaper, while my friends' boys will find any inanimate object and pretend it has the power to kill.) In addition, girls have an accelerated occipital lobe, which allows her brain to take in more sensory data than the male brain. (Think men and communication.) Finally, he describes a part of the brain called the *hippocampus*, which is another area of the brain that develops differently in girls and boys. Its main job is memory storage, and it is much larger in females than it is in males. Gurian uses an example of a young boy and a young girl being asked by their parents to do three things around the house: clean up their rooms, take out the garbage, and wipe the table. He said that more often than not, we will see the young girl complete the tasks with less reminding than the boy would need and that this has a lot to do with the hippocampal memory.

Isn't it possible, then, that this part of the brain has something to do with why women are more productive in the home? Isn't it possible that most women simply *care* more about household matters and that they're more inclined to do them? Take my husband and me, for example. He and I have our own bathrooms (a luxury I highly recommend and try very hard not to take for granted) and are each responsible for cleaning them. Now, you can bet that my husband will clean his bathroom maybe one time for every three times I've cleaned mine. Weeks (dare I say months?) will go by before he gets to it. Not only that, I can't remember a time when he cleaned his bathroom without my prodding him to do so. I sometimes fear that if I never said anything, his entire bathroom would turn green. My husband is not neglecting this chore in the hope that I will clean his bathroom for him. He honestly couldn't care less how clean his bathroom looks or smells. It's not that men expect women to clean up after them; it's that they just don't care.

I am never surprised at how many wives, after they ask their husbands to do a particular thing—paint a room, clean the bathroom, give baby a bath, or throw their dirty clothes in the dirty clothesbasket rather than on the floor—say they have to remind their husbands to do as they promised. Not long ago, I saw a Sears commercial that addressed this very issue. It showed a husband and wife sweating profusely in their home because their air conditioner was broken. The wife says, "They say it's going to be another scorcher," as she waves a fan in front of her face. "Did you call the guy about fixing the air conditioner?" The husband responds, "No, I have to do that." Then the wife says, "Well, can you do it today?" And the husband says, "Yeah." "When?" she asks. "Later." Then the wife comes over and sits down next to her husband, where he's reading the newspaper, and places the telephone directly in his hands. "Can you call him *now*?" she asks. The husband smiles and takes the phone. "All right, I'll call now." This commercial is obviously geared toward married couples, specifically wives, who know all too well how slow husbands are to get things done around the house. Therefore, there must be a grain of truth to Gurian's theory: that there's an inherent biological difference between men and women that causes women to be more productive in the home than men. This "inequality" doesn't mean that men are consciously disrespectful of women, as gender feminists presume. It only means they don't think the same way women do. Surely, there are husbands out there who are, shall we say, domestically challenged—and may therefore be useless at home. But most husbands today are not. Men are simply more inclined to be productive outside the home than inside. It's in their genes.

There are many women who refuse to accept that when it comes to caring for newborns, moms are the better choice. Indeed, most men are not as natural with babies as most women are. While today's men may accept that parenting is their responsibility as well—and participate in ways men before them never did—we should probably be content to leave it at that. Men and women are simply not interchangeable at this particular stage of life. "Babies need their soft, overplump, familiar-smelling, hairlessly lactating, soft-speaking mothers to coddle, coo, and soothe them into toddlerhood, when fathers become indispensable," writes Kathleen Parker in *USA Today*. She adds, "Call it hormonal, chemical, psychological, but ignore it at great risk to humanity."[13]

So am I saying that men shouldn't be expected to do their fair share of household chores and child care because of the size of their hippo-campus? Of course not. What I am saying is that we cannot deny that there are distinct differences between men and women, and that these differences are merely underscored when they become parents. None of this means that it's acceptable for men to do nothing and women to do everything; it just means that perhaps the reason most couples have always struggled with this issue—and will continue to struggle—is not because of social expectations, as Steinem and Friedan suggest, but because we cannot change nature. We simply have to compromise. Clearly, if you find yourself getting up every Saturday or Sunday morning with the baby while your husband sleeps in or drinks his coffee and reads the newspaper, or if your husband takes off for a round of golf every weekend morning, then something has to change. But just because you cook most of the dinners or change most of the diapers doesn't mean that your marriage isn't "equal."

Besides, equality in the home is largely a matter of how both men and women set things up in the beginning of their marriage. Indeed, feminists like to pretend that matters of the home are all about male dysfunction, but they are not. Both men *and women* have to do their part. While husbands need to recognize that household matters, including child care, are half their responsibility during the time in which they are home, women have to allow their husbands to do things their way. Too often women demand that their husbands do their part and then complain about the way they do it. I am not exempt from this. Whenever my husband is "in charge" of our daughter and about to take her out somewhere, I often come into the room when he's about to dress her to see what it is he thinks he's going to put on her. Invariably, it's something that doesn't match, and of course, I tell him so. But then I remember that if I want to be married to a man who is a full partner on the home front, I have to allow my daughter to walk around looking silly and just hope that no one thinks I dressed her. In other words, women have to be willing to give up some power if they want to maintain an equal partnership.

Second, women must speak up very early on in a marriage about what they expect from their husbands. Indeed, I'm convinced there are only two ways to avoid lifelong marital conflict regarding household chores and child care. The first is to marry a man who considers parenting his duty as well as yours and is used to cleaning up after himself. (In other words, don't marry a mama's boy or you'll be in for a long ride.) The second option is to train your husband. And this must begin the moment you become parents together. If you find that your husband thinks he can still live the way he did before he became a father (and many men do), then you act right away. As Ruth, a full-time mom of two toddlers put it, "Tonight my husband and I argued about who actually had time alone and who was supposed to be watching the kids. John accuses me of keeping score. But I feel that one has to remind the other when someone was lucky enough to play a 5½ hour golf game the weekend before when I didn't get one minute of alone time."[14] Ruth is right to point this out, *not* because she wants to play tit for tat but because if she never spoke up, her husband might assume that he can play golf fairly often and that Ruth doesn't mind. But many women do not speak up. They hold their feelings in, and it isn't until ten golf games later that the couple realizes that (in this case) the husband's lack of respect and maturity has become an important issue in their marriage. If women want to avoid this type of conflict, if they expect their husbands to grasp what it is they do all day, my suggestion is to *leave them alone with the children*. Not for a few hours, but for an entire day or weekend. Believe me, they'll get the message.

Finally, the question that always seems to come up among feminists is why men are not expected to stay home and raise children. (Notice, incidentally, how the question sounds like something a child would ask: "What about him? Why doesn't he have to do it?" It's as though we're complaining about *having* to do something rather than *getting* to do something. How sad for our children that we should argue about who *has* to be with them.) But the answer to their question is simple: women are the ones who *want* to raise children. The only reason we dismiss this fact (and certainly there are exceptions to the rule) is that feminists have instilled the idea that there are no real differences between men and women. But as the success of *Men Are From Mars, Women Are From Venus* proves, few people actually believe this. Furthermore, the secret of our label-sensitive society is that women are simply better at raising children. While surely there are couples for whom the roles are reversed, this does not change the fact that in the majority of cases, women are home because they *feel* they belong there. And that's a far cry from being *told* they belong there.

Another big secret about married life after a couple has children is sex. Many people don't realize the extent to which their sex lives will change, and there's a very good reason for this. Many years ago, men and women didn't have sex before marriage, so if they weren't having a lot of sex when they were married, or if it wasn't the most fulfilling sex in the world, they had nothing with which to compare it. This is no longer the case. Since most people today test the waters before marriage, they are used to having sex without the sounds of children reverberating through the house. Then people marry and have children, they find that their sex life isn't what it once was. This can be a big shock to those of us who have grown up with television and movies that make sex look like the be-all-end-all. People got it in their heads that not only should sex be exciting, it should be something we do all the time, all through our lives. Never mind that sex tends to become less passionate once a relationship has developed, that experts like Dr. Phil remind us that the kind of sex one has at the beginning of a relationship is very different from the kind of sex one has over the course of a long-term, committed relationship. People still choose to define sex solely in terms of frequency and excitement, so when the honeymoon is over, we assume there's something wrong with our relationship—or with our marriage. But if you continue to think this way, you are doomed, because even if you managed to have exciting, movie-like sex before you had children, this is very likely to change after you have children. And this has nothing whatsoever to do with the quality of your marital relationship or your sexual compatibility. It's just that sex inevitably takes a back seat to the responsibilities of adult life, particularly parenthood. Indeed, for parents of young children, sex almost has to be penciled in as if it were on a "to do" list. This isn't necessarily bad, but it is different from what we had imagined. "I suspect our expectations about sexual gratification within marriage are way out of line with what most normal human beings can be expected to deliver. Sure, there are couples who manage to make the earth move, and keep it moving for a lifetime, never straying, always inventive, ever attentive. But all the evidence suggests that the shining example such couples set is highly exceptional. Anomalous, even," writes Maushart in *Wifework*.[15]

Of course, no one wants anyone else to know that one's sex life wanes after the children come (although everyone who has children knows it), because we are all supposed to be having great sex all the time. But as Lisa Wolfe's story proves, there should be no expectation that married couples will be able to have sex as often or in the same way throughout their married lives, especially during the years of young parenthood. Indeed, how often couples have sex is of no consequence unless they are not having it at all or unless a couple's idea of frequency differs. Sex is only one component of a marriage; it does not define a marriage.

The really shocking part is that it doesn't even matter. For one thing, it is only temporary. Second, most couples find that what they thought was romantic before they had children pales in comparison to their newfound sense of romance as parents. Candlelight dinners are nice, yes. But they can't compare to the glance between a man and a woman over the head of a sleeping child. They can't compare to the rush of emotion a woman feels as she watches her husband make her child laugh. As Dale Hanson Bourke writes, "I wish [my friend] could understand how much more you can love a man who is careful always to powder the baby or who never hesitates to play 'bad guys' with his son. I think she should know that she will fall in love with her husband again for reasons she would now find very unromantic."[16] And this is perhaps one of the greatest problems in young marriages. Because we are so caught up in the here and now, in the fun and spontaneity of relationships, we overlook the romance of family. Indeed, moments of passion are often fleeting, but real love lasts forever.

It is unfortunate that women are not privy to the truths about motherhood until they are deep in the trenches. Perhaps if we knew ahead of time the power our children would have over us, the idea of making a choice between them and a career would seem rather absurd. In fact, the reason the women's movement continues to hit a brick wall is because its platform demands that women put themselves first—and yet the overwhelming majority of women discover, once they become mothers, that they no longer want to. As Bourke writes, "I want to assure [my friend] that she will eventually shed the pounds of pregnancy, but she will never feel the same way about herself, that her life, so now important, will be of less value to her once she has a child."[17]

This is the reality of motherhood. Embrace it.

~

Embracing Full-Time Motherhood

As I gazed out into the comic fog of my motherhood, I began to wonder if maybe there wasn't a
lesson in this for me. Maybe motherhood was an
opportunity to face certain things that, under normal circumstances, I'd want to avoid. Like sitting.
And just being. I realized that motherhood's commitment was an opportunity for me to peel back
some of my life's more surfacey layers and have a
peek at what I was really made of.

Laurie Wagner

B ELIEVE IT OR NOT, full-time motherhood is back in vogue.
Real, bona fide motherhood, the job that asks women to care
for their children full-time, every day, all year round. The
job in which women wake each day and tend to their children by
nursing them, bathing them, dressing them, cooking for them, cleaning up after them, playing with them, teaching them, talking to them,
disciplining them, caring for them when they're sick, keeping them
on a healthy routine, helping them with their schoolwork, hugging

them, kissing them, and making all the necessary sacrifices required to adequately care for their children. You know, that kind of mother.

It's a cultural shift that's been long in coming. "For the first time in 25 years, the proportion of working mothers with children under one year old posted a decline, to 55% in 2000 from 59% in 1998," writes Sue Shellenbarger.[1] There are several reasons for this turnaround. For one thing, the Generation x'ers have witnessed the Baby Boomers' attempt to have it all and do not want that life for themselves. "Many young women express surprising ambivalence about their working mothers' lives and are attracted to a different goal: to be with their children as they grow and not rely on babysitters, as their mothers did," writes Marie Brenner, author of *Great Dames: What I Learned From Older Women*.[2] Women have also discovered that the workplace isn't all it's cracked up to be. "I think women are beginning to feel betrayed by work. What they see at work, this identity, community, meaning, is not being found," says work historian Benjamin Hunnicutt.[3] Women have to come to realize that it makes no sense to have children if one's intention is to find them another home in which to spend the majority of their waking hours. A former working mother, Margaret Cox observes, "Before I knew I was expecting my third child, I had a kind of epiphany. Although I loved my job and had a great one, I needed to be at home for my boys. I knew I had to make a difference in their lives. I needed to raise them myself."[4] Finally, many women now accept that they do not really "have to work"—despite rampant use of this rationalization—because they recognize that having to do without some things is not the same as being poor.

Thankfully, motherhood no longer means living a life akin to that of the 1950s housewife. Not only have house dresses been replaced with work-out garb, mothers have every convenience they could ask for: dishwashers, disposable diapers, washing machines, microwaves, VCRs, cordless and hands-free phones, computers, and the Internet. The days of traditional homemaking are long gone. Women can now spend the bulk of their time enjoying their children. More important, though, women now accept that the issue of combining work and motherhood has little to do with gender (that is, a woman's "place") and everything to do with practicality and feasibility. They are also discovering, much to their surprise, that they actually like being with their children. Who would have thought that despite the hard work and sacrifice, such small, little beings could bring such pleasure and satisfaction? It appears society has kept such details hidden away.

Simply put, more and more women now recognize the enormous value—indeed, the basic necessity—of a house being a home, rather than a place to sleep and shower. They are content with the vast options women have today and place the most value on one of these: motherhood. To them, it is a profession and a privilege, not a jail sentence. Although their careers are on hold, they are multifaceted women, not beholden to a job for their happiness or self-esteem. They are certain their lives are meant for more than receiving a paycheck and that the moments of childhood come only once in a lifetime. "We want, at the end of our lives, to look back and see that what we have done amounts to more than a pile of pay stubs, that we have loved and been loved," writes Danielle Crittenden.[5]

Unfortunately, many women still haven't made the connection between their choice to have it all and their overall sense of despondency. In 1999, $500 million dollars worth of self-help books were sold.[6] *Five hundred million dollars.* It seems to me that if what Betty Friedan said were true—that raising children is a life of "empty, purposeless days"[7] and that self-fulfillment is the only path to a woman's true identity—women would be too busy being happy and fulfilled to scour the self-help section of their local bookstore. "I don't think women as a group are much happier now than they were in the 50s," says psychologist Mary Pipher.[8] Indeed they are not, and the reason for this is that Friedan's solution to the "problem that has no name" was bogus. It is good for women to be recognized for their many capabilities outside of motherhood; but the fact remains that most women do not find happiness by pursuing careers at the expense of motherhood.

Many people to whom women have turned have told them, in no uncertain terms, that it is impossible to have it all. Dr. Phil, known best for his ability to "tell it like it is," tells readers in the September 2001 edition of *O* magazine, "Life is about tough choices. I have never encountered a successful person who didn't have to sacrifice in one area of her life to be more successful in another. If you put more into your career, kids and family suffer; if you put more into family, career suffers. That's the bottom line."[9] Financial guru Suze Orman tells us that financial freedom can only be achieved by giving up certain things we want. Oprah tells us that it is through giving to others that we grow as human beings. "When you shift your focus from success to service, your work will instantly have more meaning."[10] The Dalai Lama tells us that material possessions mean nothing in the end and that true fulfillment can only be gained through sacrifice. And Gary Zukav explains that one's soul can never be at peace if we are always looking for more. In *Seat of the Soul*, he writes, "If you follow your feelings, you become aware of the different parts of yourself, and the different things they want. You cannot have all of them at once because many of them conflict. The fulfillment of one part of you creates anguish in another, or others, and you are torn."[11] It is this feeling of being torn between career and motherhood that leaves women feeling empty. Women just don't realize that grass always looks greener on the other side—but rarely is.

Career and motherhood are not equal and interchangeable. Many women have failed to find a sense of purpose in the workforce, but few women fail to find a sense of purpose at home. As Orenstein writes about the women she interviewed for her book, "Questions of career and achievement just didn't drive women the way they once had. The voice of ambition I'd heard in women had modulated from eager to conflicted to disinterested."[12] One woman tells her, "By your mid-forties you're supposed to have attained a certain level professionally, and most of us actually have. But it's just . . . so what? What are you going to do? Buy more things? Make more money?"[13] And yet, if you asked another group of women who had spent the same amount of time pursuing full-time motherhood, few—if any—would feel that their children didn't "drive them the way they once had" or that their feelings about motherhood "had modulated from eager to conflicted to disinterested." And that's because there is no comparison between one's children and one's career. Raising children will always be more satisfying and valuable than any other work we do.

In the end, many women have come to learn that the only road to happiness is a sense of place and that this sense of place cannot be found at work. John Perry Barlow defines happiness this way: "Happiness is not a solitary endeavor; it's a joint enterprise, something that can only be created by the whole. Contentment arises from a sense of family, community, and connectedness. Such virtues are in dwindling supply in America."[14] And the reason they are dwindling is that working motherhood pulls women further and further away from this goal. The faster we move and the more we do, the less time we have for family. Moreover, says Barlow, sacrifice has been underrated: "We have come to regard service as a self-suppressing obligation rather than a self-fulfilling responsibility. It doesn't have to be that way."[15]

Unfortunately, many women have yet to accept this fact. Consequently, they do not take the time to consider why they want children in the first place or what the purpose of motherhood is. Not only do they not think about the emotional and financial aspects of motherhood, they do not ask themselves if they are ready for a career change that will require them to make huge sacrifices. Women ignore these issues and go into motherhood blindly, irresponsibly. Part of the reason they can do this is that society doesn't encourage women to plan for motherhood. Women are not expected to curtail their lives to suit the needs of children—so what's to think about? According to modern-day society, motherhood only requires women to make it through pregnancy and childbirth (Have you seen the array of books on this subject?), find a "quality" caregiver, and resume life as normal. As a result, the average woman today gives very little thought to the realities of motherhood until the day her baby arrives. As Gurdon observes, "I discovered how tricky it can be for thirty-something professionals like me to immerse ourselves in domesticity when our lifelong expectations, and virtually all of our role models, are outside of it."[16]

One of the results of women not planning ahead for motherhood is that they presume their circumstances to be a matter of luck. Women are lucky to be able to conceive. They are lucky if they are able to stay home with their children. They are lucky if they have their mothers nearby. They are lucky if they have the kind of job that allows them to work from home. They are lucky if their husbands pull their weight at home. Amidst all these fortunate circumstances, it's hard to believe that there are any happy full-time mothers. But there are. For what many women don't consider is the fact that some women plan their lives around motherhood, rather than planning motherhood around their lives. Some women create a life for themselves that is conducive to raising children. "If there's a single, remarkable generational difference between the Boomers and the Gen-xers, it's that more of the younger women are now planning at this stage of their lives," writes Susan Brenna.[17]

And so can you.

Planning for motherhood requires women to start thinking about children soon after they graduate from college, the idea being that if they give motherhood at least as much attention as they do their careers—if not more—they can then strike that balance they are so desperately seeking. They can plan to have children and a career—but separately. Or they can plan to incorporate some type of work with motherhood in a way that will not interfere with their obligation to their children. Thinking about children at the age of twenty-two does not mean women need to get married. On the contrary, I think most people should wait to settle down. It does mean that they must begin thinking about their desire to raise children and the need to be out of the workforce for a short time. Maybe not for eighteen years—though this should certainly be an option—but for five or six at least.

There are three things women can do to plan for motherhood. First, choose a career that works well with motherhood. This is easier said than done, but it is easier to accomplish today than it has ever been. It is true, of course, that some careers do not offer women the flexibility they need to put their children first. In fact, it is because of the naturally conflicting natures of career and motherhood that women have dominated more flexible fields like nursing and teaching. Feminists would like us to believe that the reason women have chosen these professions is that men don't believe they can compete in the cutthroat, male dominated business world. It never seems to have occurred to them that perhaps women don't want to compete in that world because they want to be mothers, first and foremost, and know that there were only a few careers that allow them to accomplish this goal. In any case, today there are many more options. Discrimination is defunct; part-time, flex-time, and job-sharing are "in"; and men are doing more household work than ever before. And then, of course, there are advances in technology, which offer women a great opportunity to combine career and motherhood. Indeed, more and more women have started their own businesses from home, which is an ideal arrangement for raising children.

Nevertheless, the fact remains that some careers just won't be an option for women—particularly the powerful and lucrative ones. We can choose them, if we wish; but not without ramifications. What's difficult about this, of course, is that it flies in the face of feminism. That is, women can't really do or be whatever they want—as men can—because of sheer biology. Becoming a doctor or a big-shot attorney, for example, will inevitably pose a problem for women who plan to have children. This is the reason Susan Stevens of Birmingham, Alabama, made a conscious choice to become a teacher rather than a doctor. "I'd be 30 before I was finished with medical school," she tells *Time* magazine.[18] The same holds true for a businesswoman who wants to rise to the top. As Robert Reich observes, "If you want to remain on the fast track, you have to work late with customers and clients, be available at all hours, develop your contacts and connections, and stay abreast of new developments."[19]

While some women are able to accept that there will be career limitations if they want to become mothers, others cannot, and remain committed to the idea that they can juggle high-powered careers and children. As Judith Regan, publisher of ReganBooks, recounts in *O* magazine, after many years of her having no time for her children, her teenage son tells her that he doesn't want to spend a week's vacation with her. "It's too late. I'm all grown up. You missed my childhood." Regan adds, "It's true. I've failed him. And I know it."[20] Unfortunately, such experiences aren't enough to convince women that there's no such thing as having it all. I guess working mothers believe that they can succeed where Regan failed. Yet Regan didn't fail because she wasn't a good enough juggler. If, as she says, she did fail, then it was because of the natural conflict between her two jobs, mother and publisher. But most working mothers are not as forthcoming as Regan. Despite their failure to make it work, many will insist that they have made it work: "My children are thriving in day care" or "I know I'm missing a lot, but it's my choice. I'm a better mom for working." And they say it again and again, in the hope that one day they'll be convinced.

The second thing women can do to plan for motherhood is to plan to live near their parents or siblings. This is very important, much more important than today's women realize. Unlike women in past generations, many women now venture far away from their homes. They no longer go to college to find husbands and return home to marry them. They go to college to develop their own interests, and then move wherever their first job takes them. As a result, women settle in areas of the country that are often far away from their hometowns. And while this can work out well when women are young and childless, it becomes a real problem when they have children. Indeed, many women come to realize that they cannot—and do not want to—raise children without the help of their families. "Having a baby makes a lot of people want to be near their families," says Alice Domar, author of *Self-Nurture*.[21]

Full-time motherhood is a job that demands the help and support of others, and it is critical that women have this support. When they don't, their marriages suffer; and when their marriages suffer, their children suffer. The reason mothers in previous generations did not struggle with the same sense of exasperation that today's mothers do is that they had extended family members around to help them and because most of their friends were home as well. Today's women, on the other hand, are isolated, and many return to the workforce out of sheer frustration.

Third, and most important, women should be responsible with their finances. This means women must save, not spend, the money they make prior to motherhood. Unfortunately, women have failed to do this; and their choice has, in a sense, caused women's liberation to backfire. That is, women wanted to be successful irrespective of men and children—and we are. But with this freedom comes responsibility, and many women are not holding up their end of the bargain. Happy to grab freedom with both hands, they do not think they have to set themselves up for the future. Women can't have it both ways. If we want to be "equal" with men, then we have to save and invest our money, as they are expected to do, rather than spend it. While women may not feel any different from men when they work alongside them in the workforce, they certainly don't feel the financial pressure that men do. Biology will once again separate the men from the women, because somewhere in the back of women's minds—way, way back—they know they can expect men to carry the financial burden. Someday they plan to have children, and while they know have the option to become working mothers, they still feel that it is within their rights to opt out of the workforce should they choose to. Men don't have this option. Or at least, they don't feel as if they do; and most men don't want this option anyway. The problem is that many women today go into debt before they have children. They buy things they cannot afford or sign mortgages that require two incomes. These are the women who find themselves in financial difficulty when they have children. They are the women who end up telling people that they "have to work." But they did have a choice; they just weren't responsible.

Now that we women have achieved what we set out to achieve, it is time we begin to focus more on family and prepare for being, at some point, out of the workforce for a time. Part of the reason for delaying motherhood is so that we can establish financial independence, right? Well, you can't be independent if you don't save what you earn. If you spend money as you make it, when you do get married, you're no better off than you were before you began working. More important, if you plan to have children and want to stay home with them, then the only option you have—other than marrying a highly successful man, which I wouldn't recommend because he won't be home very much—is to postpone motherhood and save your money. Then marry a modestly successful family man and add your savings to the pot. That way, you can be a full-time mom when the time comes. And maybe then we will hear no more of that favorite line of working mothers: "You're so lucky. I wish I could afford to stay home." Luck has nothing to do with it. It really is possible for most women to be home with their children—if they honestly want to be. And if they plan ahead.

It's time to shift our paradigm. Women must begin to view motherhood as something they get to do rather than something they have to squeeze into their hectic career lives. Motherhood is a career, not a sideline occupation. As one woman tells Peggy Orenstein, "The kids are now my work. They are my job. And in the same way that I was a perfectionist at work and cared a great deal about the product and about winning and all of those things, that has been translated over to my kids."[22] Furthermore, women have plenty of time to pursue their own interests. Not only do we have time to focus on ourselves before we have children, we have the rest of our lives—after our children are grown—to become self-absorbed again. "Just as the young never really understand, or believe, that there is a long, long time stretching ahead of them in which to do all the things they want, so many young mothers continue to feel that if they don't move on the question of career now, the world will simply pass them by," writes Midge Decter.[23] It makes little sense to eschew the power and flexibility that comes from raising children solely because we fear who we might become without our jobs. There is no reason to try to do everything at once. We can afford to take time out of our forty-year careers to raise our children. Yes, putting one's career on the back burner may put some of us at a disadvantage when we enter the workforce again, but not doing so will put us at a disadvantage with our children—and our souls. Motherhood changes who we are. It is a gift, a chance to become a better person. What could be more liberating than that?

Contrary to what the women's movement would have us believe, the traditional family structure is not something that holds women down. The traditional family structure simply keeps women from having to worry about producing an income while they work on the most important job of their lives. And most husbands—even if they keep it to themselves—want to support them. One of the main reasons my generation has not been successful with marriage and family is that we do not view the family as a permanent unit, with two people working toward the same goal. Today's women are taught to be responsible for themselves, first and foremost, so that in case their marriages dissolve, they will have well-paying jobs. But this philosophy has failed.

Today, many men no longer value, or even understand, the purpose of full-time motherhood. And why would they? Women have been dismissive of its economic and social value for the past forty years. We have asserted that raising children is somehow beneath us, that it's boring, and that it holds less value than producing an income—so now men have even less regard for motherhood than they did before. "The breadwinner ethic provided real stability for many in our society, and a generally shared idea for how to live, how to connect, how to build families," writes Philipson.[24] This has, in fact, been the greatest irony of all. For one of the goals of the women's movement was to get men more involved in the home and show them the amount of work involved in raising children. Instead, we joined men in their world, becoming breadwinners instead of mothers, thereby leading even fewer people to appreciate the work that goes into motherhood. In the end, then, all we've done is push both parents out of the home. I would hardly call this progress.

It is abundantly clear that the philosophy of the last several decades—this Everyone For Himself philosophy—has failed. As the current divorce rate shows, there is no longer any incentive to settle down. This is why it is imperative that we re-evaluate the purpose of the traditional family, with one parent at home and one parent in the workforce. Until we do, Americans will never again be successful in raising strong families. It seems to me that the secret to making sense of career and motherhood is to see beyond the here and now, beyond our immediate wants and desires. If I had given up and gone back to work when my daughter was in her first year of life, merely because the transition was so jarring and her crying incessant, I would never have known the joy and sense of fulfillment I know now. It is because I stuck it out, waited patiently (a trait I needed to learn anyway), and worked hard every day to develop a relationship with my daughter that we share a strong bond. Does this mean she will always be the perfect child or that I will never struggle as a parent simply because I stayed home with her? Of course not. But it does mean that she knows I will be here for her tomorrow. And the next day. And the day after that. It means that she can count on me, not to be a perfect mother, but a stable force in her life. Most important, it means that she knows I consider her worth my time and attention.

And this will mark her soul for a lifetime.

Afterword

⁓

Only through acknowledging the complementarity of work outside the home and work in the home—and the dependence of the former sphere on the latter—can we hope to arrive at equity and due deference for the true heroes and heroines of our society: the men and women for whom family comes first.

Brian C. Robertson

AFTER I COMPLETED THE MANUSCRIPT that would become this book, several interesting things happened. To begin with, the following headlines appeared in magazines and newspapers across the country: "Babies vs. Career" (*Time*, April 2002), "Putting Family First" (*People*, April 2002), "More moms make kids the career of their choice"(*USA Today*, March 2002), and "The Importance of Being Mom" (*Wall Street Journal*, March 2002). In addition, a book entitled *Creating a Life: Professional Women and the Quest for Children*, by Sylvia Ann Hewlett, was published. It addresses the reality of a woman's biological clock and urges women to plan for motherhood well in advance, making all the necessary modifications to accommodate this awesome task. And finally, two resignations made national headlines. One was former Massachusetts governor Jane Swift, who finally came to terms with her inability to be the governor of a state and raise three children under five (including one set of twins) simultaneously, and the other was Karen Hughes, former advisor to President Bush, who announced that she too was resigning because of family obligations.

I'd like to say there's a pattern developing, one which proves that maybe, just maybe, we're finally getting it: Women can't have it all—not at the same time. And yet there remains a force holding back the tide. The moment stories about women putting family first become public, we're swamped with feminist rhetoric. Hewlett received scores of attacks from gender feminists, who claim she wants to send women back to the dark ages (just as they'll say about me), when all Hewlett did is point out the truth: women can't always do what they want, whenever they want—because their bodies have an agenda of their own.

I find it fascinating how many women continue to ignore the truth about work and family, but the reason they do is obvious. Mothers who choose to work full-time outside the home and place their children in other people's care have a vested interest in denying the truth, because if they *were* to face the fact that women can't have it all, they would have to take a second look at the choice they've made—and most are unable to do this. So rather than face their demons, they get angry at those who dare to speak the truth.

Yet at some point, every working mother will have The Epiphany, reminding her that there are consequences for choosing work over family. For no matter how much women wish it weren't true, the world will never revolve around our needs as individuals. Every choice we make directly affects those near us. As William and Wendy Dreskin observe, "There are very few actions a person can take that truly affect no one else. The basic problem with the looking-out-for-number-one philosophy is that it ignores the fact that we are all social beings living in this society. Responsibility and guilt are not just 'old-fashioned morality' but relate to the basic trust necessary for peaceful social interaction. Without expectations and obligations of any kind, the social fabric would be torn without repair."

And there's no question about it: Working motherhood, on a mass scale, damages our social fabric. Unfortunately, as a society we have yet to accept this fact—which continues to amaze me. After all, we love to watch movies and read books about people who have learned the lessons of life. We bask in the advice of professionals and in books like *Tuesdays with Morrie*, in which a dying man shares his wisdom with a former student. We hear their message, yet we continue to live in the moment. Tomorrow will never come, we think. But one day when we're old and gray, we will wonder not only where the time went, but what we accomplished. No matter how much power we have or how important we think we are at work, we are still replaceable. But we are not replaceable to our children, and there is no greater power than this.

Full-time motherhood will never go out of style. It may be questioned. It may be modified. But it will always be revered by those who understand it. Some things in life are innate, natural. And the essence of nature is that no matter how much we try to change it, no matter how much we *want* to change it, it will reassert itself. Mother Nature has known this forever. We'd be wise to listen.

Notes

≋

Introduction

1   Ann Crittenden, *The Price of Motherhood: Why the Most Important Job in the World Is Still the Least Valued* (New York: Metropolitan Books, 2001), 30.
2   Bernard Goldberg, *Bias: A CBS Insider Exposes How the Media Distort the News.* (Washington D.C.: Regnery Publishing, Inc., 2002), 169.

MYTH #1
"Men Can Have It All. Why Shouldn't We?"

1   Christina Hoff Sommers, *Who Stole Feminism? How Women Have Betrayed Women* (New York: Simon and Schuster, 1994), 17.
2   Sommers writes that "gender feminists" believe all our institutions perpetuate male dominance.
3   Sommers, 17.
4   F. Carolyn Graglia, *Domestic Tranquility: A Brief Against Feminism* (Dallas: Spence Publishing, 1998), 4.
5   Betty Friedan, *The Feminine Mystique* (New York: W.W. Norton & Company, 2001), xv.
6   Ibid.
7   Ibid., xvi.
8   Midge Decter, *An Old Wife's Tale: My Seven Decades In Love and War* (New York: Regan Books, 2001), 92.
9   Friedan, 317.
10 Ann Crittenden, 13.
11 Interview with Marlo Thomas on *The Phil Donahue Show* (1970s), as seen on Lifetime television.
12 Megan Rutherford, "When Mother Stays Home," *Time.com* (October 16, 2000).

13   Sylvia Ann Hewlett, *Creating a Life: Professional Women and the Quest for Children* (New York: Hyperion, 2002), 119-20.
14   Lisa Schiffren, "Family First," *Wall Street Journal* (March 19, 1998): A18.
15   Decter, 51.
16   Peggy Orenstein, *Flux: Women on Sex, Work, Love, Kids, & Life In a Half-Changed World* (New York: Anchor Books, 2000), 17.
17   Susan Douglas and Meredith Michaels, *The Mommy Myth: The Idealization of Motherhood and How It Has Undermined Women* (New York: Free Press, 2004), 34
18   Anna Quindlen, "Playing God On No Sleep," *Newsweek* (July 2, 2001): 64.

MYTH #2

"I Could Never Stay Home Full-Time."

1   Friedan, 377.
2   Danielle Crittenden, *What Our Mothers Didn't Tell Us: Why Happiness Eludes the Modern Woman* (New York: Touchstone, 1999), 121.
3   Decter, 193.
4   Telephone Interview (October 2001)
5   Rutherford, "When Mother Stays Home"
6   Ibid.
7   Ann Crittenden, 72.
8   United States Census Bureau Current Population Survey, March 1997.
9   Lisa Collier Cool, "Raising Kids in a World of Internet Speed," *Child* (August 2001): 76.
10   Linda Burton, Janet Dittmer, and Cheri Loveless, *What's a Smart Woman Like You Doing At Home?* (Vienna, VA: Family and Home Network, 1992), 132.
11   Meghan Cox Gurdon, "She's Back!" *The Women's Quarterly* (Spring 1998)
12   Lisa Belkin, "The Opt-Out Revolution," *New York Times Magazine* (October 26, 2003): 44.
13   Gurdon, "She's Back!"
14   Sir Wilfred Grenfell in *O, The Oprah Magazine* (May 2001): 91.
15   Gurdon, "She's Back!"
16   Hewlett, 83-4.
17   Burton, Dittmer, and Loveless, 63.
18   Joan K. Peters, *When Mothers Work: Loving Our Children Without Sacrificing Ourselves* (New York: Addison Wesley Longman, 1997), xiii.
19   Danielle Crittenden, 119.
20   Maria Shriver, *Ten Things (I Wish I'd Known — Before I Went Out into the Real World)*. (New York: Warner Books, 2000), 81.
21   Friedan, 381.
22   Susan Chira, *A Mother's Place: Choosing Work and Family Without Guilt or Blame* (New York: Harper Collins, 1998), xiii.
23   Ibid., 46.
24   Ibid., 23.
25   Orenstein, 33.
26   Arlie Russell Hochschild, *The Time Bind: When Work Becomes Home & Home Becomes Work* (New York: Metropolitan, 1997), 186.

27 Shannon Brownlee and Matthew Miller, "Lies Parents Tell Themselves About Why They Work," *U.S News & World Report* (May 12, 1997): 59.

28 Goldberg, 61.

29 Ibid., 59.

30 Ibid., 167.

31 Freidan, xv.

1 Jennifer Roback Morse, "Why the Market Can't Raise Our Children for Us," *American Enterprise* (May/June 1998).

2 Danielle Crittenden, 132-33.

3 Brownlee and Miller, 60.

4 Ibid.

5 Peggy Orenstein, "Will Your Child Suffer If You Work?" *Redbook* (August 2001): 55.

6 Stephen Covey, *The 7 Habits of Highly Effective Families* (New York: Golden Books, 1997), 118.

7 Ibid.

8 Brownlee and Miller, 59.

9 Decter, 50.

10 Oprah Winfrey, Interview with the Dalai Lama, *O, The Oprah Magazine* (August 2001): 123.

11 Robert Reich, *The Future of Success* (New York: Alfred Knopf, 2001), 175.

12 Anna Quindlen, *A Short Guide to a Happy Life* (New York: Random House, 2000), 38.

13 *Good Morning America*, June 19, 2002; Daniel McGinn, "Maxed Out!" *Newsweek* (August 27, 2001): 34.

14 Thomas J. Stanley, Ph.D. and William D. Danko, Ph.D., *The Millionaire Next Door: The Surprising Secrets of America's Wealthy* (New York: Simon & Schuster, 1996), 1.

15 Reich, 226.

16 Sue Shellenbarger, "In Cataclysmic Times, Workers Need Room to Rethink Priorities," *The Wall Street Journal* (September 19, 2001): B1.

17 Burton, Dittmer, and Loveless, 99.

1 Sue Shellenbarger, "You *Can* Find the Time," *Parade Magazine* (August 5, 2001): 10.

2 Judith Regan, "Quality Time," *O, The Oprah Magazine* (April 2001): 92.

3 Karen Levine, "Family Time Band," *Parents* (April 1998): 124.

4 Ibid.

5 Interview with Laura Pappano in *Radcliffe Quarterly* (Summer 2001): 21.

6 Lisa Belkin, *Life's Work* (New York: Simon & Schuster, 2002), 120

7 Susan Maushart, *The Mask of Motherhood: How Becoming a Mother Changes Our Lives and Why We Never Talk About It* (New York: Penguin Books, 1999), 200.

8 Alison Ashton, "When It's Work vs. Family, Work Usually Wins," *Working Mother* (December 2001): 10.

9   Katherine Wyse Goldman, *Working Mothers 101: How to Organize Your Life, Your Children, and Your Career to Stop Feeling Guilty and Start Enjoying It All* (New York: Cliff Street Books, 1998), 4, 157.

10   Ibid., 159.

11   Ibid., 157-158.

12   Ibid., 160.

13   Oprah Winfrey, "Heart to Heart," *O, The Oprah Magazine* (October 2001): 39.

14   Ann Crittenden, 22.

15   Friedan, xv.

16   Friedan, xxiv.

17   Friedan, xxiii.

18   Rhonda Kruse Nordin and Dwenda K. Gjerdingen, *After the Baby: Making Sense of Marriage After Childbirth* (Dallas: Taylor Publishing, 2000), 87.

19   Levine, 124.

20   Laura Pappano, *The Connection Gap: Why Americans Feel So Alone* (New Brunswick: Rutgers University Press, 2001), 204.

21   Ibid.

22   Ibid., 203.

23   Betsy Currier Beacom, "Mom Bonds," *Working Mother* (June 2001): 51.

24   Ibid., 52.

25   Orenstein, 201.

26   Katy Abel, "Time Well Spent: Working Moms and Kids," *Family Education.com* .

27   Reich, 217.

28   Goldman, 18.

29   Ibid.

30   Ibid.

31   Hochschild, 212.

32   Ibid.

33   Orenstein, 55.

34   Annie Finnigan, "The Inside Story," *Working Mother* (October 2001): 66.

35   Arlie Hochschild, *The Second Shift: Working Parents and the Revolution At Home* (New York: Viking Press, 1989), 97.

36   Nordin and Gjerdingen, 85.

37   Tara Parker-Pope and Kyle Pope, "A Firestorm Over Stay-at-Home Moms," *St. Louis Post Dispatch* (February 25, 2001): E4.

38   Shriver, 78.

39   Ibid.

40   Chira, xv.

41   "How do we make it work?" ed., *St. Louis Post-Dispatch* (October 26, 2000).

42

43   Goldman, 57.

44   Ibid, 175.

45   Shellenbarger, 10.

46   Ibid.

MYTH #5
"I'm a Better Mom for Working."

1   Susan Caminiti, "Work and Family," *Parenting* (May 2001): 59.
2   Penelope Leach, "The Most Important Bond," *Child* (October 2001): 64.
3   Barbara Kantrowitz and Pat Wingert, "The Parent Trap," *Newsweek* (January 29, 2001): 49.
4   Personal Interview, May 2001.
5   Personal Interview, August 2001.
6   Personal Interview, December 2001; "No more 9 to 5," *Minnesota Monthly* (January 2002).
7   Ron Taffel, *The Second Family: How Adolescent Power Is Changing the American Family* (New York: St. Martin's Press, 2001), 19.
8   Ibid., 20.
9   Inda Schaenen, *The 7 O'Clock Bedtime* (New York: ReganBooks, 2001): xii.
10   Ibid., 5.
11   Dr. Marc Weissbluth, "Sleeping With Ease," *The Today Show* (November 16, 2001)
12   Jodi Mindell, Ph.D., "How Much Sleep Does Your Child Need?" *BabyCenter.com*
13   Diane Fisher, Ph.D., Testimony, "Pre to Three: Policy Implications of Child Brain Development," June 5, 1997.
14   Richard Ferber, *Solve Your Child's Sleep Problems* (New York: Fireside Books, 1985), 44.
15   Weissbluth, "Sleeping With Ease"
16   Schaenen, 134.
17   Reich, 159.
18. Goldman, 51.
19   Ibid., 52.
20   Nanci Hellmich, "Fingers point to Mom for picky eaters," *USA Today* (February 25, 2002): 13B.
21   Ibid.
22   Shannon Brownlee, "Too Heavy, Too Young," *Time* (January 21, 2002): 88.
23   Ibid.
24   Cynthia Billhartz, "Taste Buds in Training," *St. Louis Post Dispatch* (August 12, 2001): EV1.
25   Brownlee, 89.
26   Billhartz, EV1.
27   Michael Gurian, *The Wonder of Girls: Understanding the Hidden Nature of Our Daughters* (New York: Pocket Books, 2002), 114.
28   Leonard Pitts Jr., "Parents Have to Learn They Can't Be Playmates," *St. Louis Post-Dispatch* (July 28, 2001): 29.
29   Brazelton, T. Berry, M.D. and Greenspan, Stanley I. , M.D. *The Irreducible Needs of Children* (Massachusetts: Perseus Publishing, 2000), 146.
30   Gurian, 122.
31   Brazelton and Greenspan, 154.
32   Ibid.
33   Gurdon, "She's Back!"

34   Susan Sherrod, "Parental involvement, support are key to a child's success in school," *Naples Daily News* (January 20, 2002): B3.

35   Melissa Kantor, "Whose Homework Is It Anyway?" *Working Mother* (November 2001): 68

36   Sal Severe, Ph.D., *How To Behave So Your Children Will Too* (New York: Viking Press, 2000), 93.

37   Katie O'Connor, *The Ladue News* (March 2001).

38   Interview with Melinda Southern, *The Oprah Show* (October 18, 2000).

39   Amy Dickinson, "Must-See TV?" *Time* (November 29, 1999): 114.

40   Schaenen, 120.

41   Naomi Freundlich, *Parents* (October 2003):138.

42   Lisa Sharkey, "A Month Without TV," *Child* (October 2001): 92.

43   Ibid., 94.

44   Yonason Goldson, "Turn off the Tube, Turn on Your Mind," *St. Louis Post-Dispatch* (April 21, 2002): B3.

45   Schaenen, 24.

46   Anna Quindlen, "Doing Nothing is Something" *Time* (May 13, 2002): 76.

47   Mary Manz Simon, "Parents need to be wary of overscheduling children, experts say," *St. Louis Post Dispatch* (November 27, 2000): C3.

48   Schaenen, 25.

49   Michele Orecklin, "Off the Couch," *People* (April 15, 2002): 83.

MYTH #6
"My Children Just Love *Day Care."*

1   Covey, 119.

2   Chira., 164.

3   Ibid., 165.

4   Ibid.

5   Fisher, "Pre to Three"

6   Karl Zinsmeister, "The Problem With Day Care," *American Enterprise* (May/June 1998)

7   Clark Gable to Vivien Leigh, *Gone With The Wind* (1939).

8   Chira, 130.

9   Hope Edelman, *Mother of My Mother* (New York: The Dial Press, 1999), 40.

10   Karl Zinsmeister, "The Problem With Day Care."

11   Greenspan, 18.

12   Goldman, 72.

13   Karl Zinsmeister, "The Problem With Day Care."

14   Burton, Dittmer, and Loveless, 49.

15   Nancy Hall, "Right Nanny, Wrong Time," *Working Mother* (July/August, 2001): 74.

16   Orenstein, 192.

17   Interview with Ellen Galinsky, *The Today Show* (October 16, 2000).

18   Fisher, "Pre to Three."

19   Ibid.

20   Ibid.

21   Burton, Dittmer, and Loveless, 150.

22 Jay Belsky, NICHD Study (April 2001).

23 Interview with Marion Wright Edelman, *CBS Evening News with Dan Rather* (2001).

24 Steve Farkas, "Necessary Compromises: How Parents, Employers, and Children's Advocates View Child Care Today," *Public Agenda Online* (August 2000)

25 Ellen Galinsky, *Ask the Children: What America's Children Really Think About Working Parents* (New York: William Morrow & Co., 1999), 332.

26 Ibid., 341.

27 Greenspan, Diane Rehm.

28 Meghan Mutchler Deerin, "Shedding light on the day care doom and gloom," *The Chicago Tribune* (July 15, 2001): 6.

29 "Independence Takes Form," *Loving Your Child Every Step of the Way* from *American Baby*, 47.

30 Zinsmeister, "The Problem With Day Care."

31 Ibid.

32 Burton, Dittmer, and Loveless, 64.

33 Betty Holcomb, *Not Guilty! The Good News for Working Mothers* (New York: Simon & Schuster, 1998), 208.

34 Fisher, "Pre to Three."

35 Holcomb, 20.

36 Gayle Peterson, "Stay-at-home mom frustrated with media," *iVillage.com*.

37 Ibid.

38 Ibid.

39 William and Wendy Dreskin, *The Day Care Decision* (New York: M. Evans and Company, Inc., 1983), 50.

40 Harriet Brown, "Who's Watching Our Children?" *Parenting.com* (June/July 1999)

41 Danielle Crittenden, 139.

MYTH #7
"I Have It All Planned Out."

1   Maushart, *The Mask of Motherhood*, 2, 7.

2   Laurie Wagner, *Expectations* (San Francisco: Chronicle Books, 1998), 44.

3   Valerie Bertinelli, Lifetime Interview

4   Susan Maushart, *Wifework* (New York: Bloomsbury, 2001), 15.

5   Pepper Schwartz, Ph.D., "Love is not all you need," *Psychology Today* (May/June 2002): 57.

6   Maushart, *Wifework*, 188.

7   Gurian, 107.

8   Nordin and Gjerdingen, 15.

9   Decter, xiv.

10 Diane Sollee, *Smartmarriages.com*

11 Lisa Wolfe, "48 Hours," *O, The Oprah Magazine* (October 2001): 284.

12 Sabra, full-time mom from Tequesta, Florida, in *Welcome Home* (Mothers At Home)

13 Kathleen Parker, "Stay home, governor, while your girls are babies," *USA Today* (May 2001): 1D.

14   Personal Interview, November 2001.

15   Maushart, *Wifework*, 240.

16   Dale Hanson Bourke, "Things Your Mother Never Told You About Motherhood," *New Woman* (March 1990): 152.

17   Ibid.

1   Sue Shellenbarger, "As More Employees Quit Jobs for Kids, One Couple's Tale," *The Wall Street Journal* (November 14, 2001): B1.

2   Marie Brenner, "Not Their Mothers' Choices," *Newsweek* (August 13, 2001): 48.

3   Erin Hayes, "Women Seeking Balance Between Work, Family," *ABCNews.com* (June 7, 2001)

4   Personal Interview, December 2001

5   Danielle Crittenden, 73.

6   Statistic reported on the *CBS Nightly News*, 2000.

7   Friedan, 314.

8   Hayes, "Women Seeking Balance"

9   Dr. Phil McGraw, "Tell It Like It Is,"*O, The Oprah Magazine* (September 2001): 60.

10   Oprah Winfrey, "What I Know For Sure," *O, The Oprah Magazine* (September 2001), 301.

11   Gary Sukav, *Seat of the Soul* (New York: Fireside, 1990), 137.

12   Orenstein, 214.

13   Ibid.

14   John Perry Barlow, "The Pursuit of Emptiness: Why Americans Have Never Been a Happy Bunch," *Forbes* (December 3, 2001): 97.

15   Ibid.

16   Gurdon, "She's Back!"

17   Susan Brenna, "The New Generation Gap," *Parenting.com* (March 1999)

18   James Poniewozik, "The Cost of Starting Families First," *Time* (April 15, 2002): 58.

19   Reich, 163.

20   Judith Regan, "Quality Time," *O, The Oprah Magazine* (April 2001): 92.

21   Monica Bernstein, "What a Difference a Baby Makes," *American Baby.com* (November 2001): 70.

22   Orenstein, 176.

23   Decter, 58.

24   Philipson, 41.

A NOTE ON THE AUTHOR

Suzanne Venker is a 1990 graduate of Boston University and a former middle school English teacher. A writer and full-time mother, she lives in St. Louis.

This book was designed and set into type
by Mitchell S. Muncy,
with cover design by Sam Torode,
and printed and bound
by Phoenix Color Corp.,
Hagerstown, Maryland.

℃

The text face is Minion Multiple Master,
designed by Robert Slimbach
and issued in digital form by Adobe Systems,
Mountain View, California, in 1991.

℃

The paper is acid-free and is of archival quality.

37